PINTER

A BIBLIOGRAPHY

**his works and occasional writings with a comprehensive checklist
of criticism and reviews of the London Productions**

Compiled by Rudiger Imhof

Second Full Revised Edition

London and Los Angeles
TQ PUBLICATIONS LTD.
1976

First Published 1975
Second Revised Edition 1976

c   Rüdiger Imhof 1975 and 1976

ISBN 0 904844 06 4

Theatrefacts Supplement
Bibliography Series No. 1
Edited by Simon Trussler

Published by TQ Publications Ltd., 44 Earlham Street, London WC2
Published in the USA by the Division of Drama, University of Southern California

Cover Designed, Typeset and Printed by the Service Departments of
The Institute for Research in Art and Technology Ltd., London

THE WORKS

PLAYS

The Basement
In *Tea Party and Other Plays* (London: Methuen, 1967); and in *The Lover, Tea Party, The Basement* (New York: Grove Press, 1970).

The Birthday Party
London: Encore Publishing Company, 1959; London: French's Acting Edition, 1959; in *The Birthday Party and Other Plays* (London: Methuen, 1960); and in *The Birthday Party and The Room* (New York: Grove Press, 1961); in: Harold Clurman (ed.), *Seven Plays of the Modern Theatre* (New York, 1967); in: Willis Hall and Keith Waterhouse (eds.), *Writers' Theatre* (London, 1967), pp. 69-77.

The Caretaker
London: Methuen, 1960; in *The Caretaker and The Dumb Waiter* (New York: Grove Press, 1961) and in *1961/62 Best Plays* ed. Henry Hewes (New York; Toronto, 1962), repr. 1974 *The Caretaker* (Frankfurt/a.M., Berlin, Munich: Diesterweg, 1975).

The Collection
In *The Collection and The Lover* (London: Methuen, 1963); London: French's Acting Edition, 1963; *Three Plays* (New York: Grove Press, 1962) and in *1962/63 Best Plays* ed. Henry Hewes (New York; Toronto 1963).

The Dumb Waiter
In *The Birthday Party and Other Plays* (London: Methuen, 1960); repr. 1973 London: French's Acting Edition, 1960; *The Caretaker and The Dumb Waiter* (New York: Grove Press, 1961): *New English Dramatists 3*, ed. Tom Maschler (Harmondsworth: Penguin, 1961); and in *Twentieth Century Drama: England, Ireland, the United States* ed. R. Cohn and B. Dukore (New York, 1966); in *The Room and The Dumb Waiter* (London: Methuen, 1966); *The Dumb Waiter* (Frankfurt/a.M., Berlin, Munich: Diesterweg, 1975).

The Dwarfs
In *A Slight Ache and Other Plays* (London: Methuen, 1961); and in *Three Plays* (New York: Grove Press, 1962).

The Homecoming
London: Methuen, 1965. repr. 1973 London: French's Acting Edition, 1965. New York: Grove Press, 1966, and in *Best Plays* ed. Otis L. Guernsey (New York; Toronto, 1967).

Landscape
In *Landscape and Silence* (London: Methuen, 1969; New York: Grove Press, 1970).

The Lover
In *The Collection and The Lover* (London: Methuen, 1963); repr. 1973
London: French's Acting Edition, 1964; and in *The Lover, Tea Party,
The Basement* (New York: Grove Press, 1967).

Monologue
London: Covent Garden Press, 1973

Night
In *Landscape and Silence* (London: Methuen, 1969; New York: Grove
Press, 1970.

A Night Out
London: French's Acting Edition, 1961; in *A Slight Ache and Other
Plays* (London: Methuen, 1966 repr. 1973); *A Night Out, Night
School, Revue Sketches* (New York: Grove Press, 1968); and in *The
Personal Conflict* ed. John Hodgson (London: Methuen, 1972).

Night School
In *Tea Party and Other Plays* (London: Methuen, 1967); and in *A Night
Out, Night School, Revue Sketches* (New York: Grove Press, 1968).

Old Times
London: Methuen, 1971. New York: Grove Press, 1971.

The Room
London: French's Acting Edition, 1960; in *The Birthday Party and
Other Plays* (London: Methuen, 1960); and in *The Birthday Party and
The Room* (New York: Grove Press 1961); *The Room and The Dumb
Waiter* (London: Methuen, 1966 repr. 1973).

A Slight Ache
London: French's Acting Edition, 1961; in *A Slight Ache and Other
Plays* (London: Methuen, 1961); and in *Three Plays* (New York: Grove
Press, 1962).

Tea Party
In *Tea Party and Other Plays* (London: Methuen, 1967); and in
The Lover, Tea Party, The Basement (New York: Grove Press, 1967).

No Man's Land
(London: Methuen, 1975), and *The New Review*, II, 13 (April 1975),
pp. 3-18.

REVUE SKETCHES

'Trouble in the Works', 'The Black and White', 'Request Stop', 'Last to Go', and 'Applicant' in *A Slight Ache and Other Plays* (London: Methuen, 1961); and in *A Night Out, Night School, Revue Sketches* (New York: Grove Press, 1968). These, and aditionally 'Interview' and 'That's All, That's Your Trouble', in *The Dwarfs and Eight Revue Sketches* (New York: Dramatists Plays Service. 'Dialogue for Three', in *Stand*, VI, 3 (1963). 'Special Offer', in Arnold P. Hinchliffe, *Harold Pinter* (New York: Twayne, 1967).

SCREENPLAYS

Five Screenplays (London: Methuen, 1971) contains the screenplays for *The Servant* (based on the novel by Robin Maugham); *The Pumpkin Eater* (based on the novel by Penelope Mortimer); *The Quiller Memorandum* (based on the novel *The Berlin Memorandum* by Adam Hall); *Accident* (based on the novel by Nicholas Mosley); and *The Go-Between* (based on the novel by L.P. Hartley).

POEMS

'Afternoon', *Twentieth Century*, 169 (February 1961), p. 218.

'All of That', *Times Literary Supplement*, LXIX (1970), p. 1436.

'Chandeliers and Shadows', *Poetry London*, 19 (August 1950).

'European Revels', *Poetry London*, 20 (November 1950).

'Later', *The New Review*, II, 23 (February 1976) p. 26

'New Year in the Midlands', *Poetry London*, 19 (August 1950).

'One a Story, Two a Death', *Poetry London*, 22 (Summer 1951).

Poems, ed. Alan Clodd (London: Enitharmon Press, 1968).

Poems (London: Enitharmon Press, 1971).

'Rural Idyll', *Poetry London*, 20 (November 1950).

SHORT STORIES

'The Examination', in *The Collection and the Lover* (London: Methuen, 1963).

'Tea Party', *Playboy*, XII, 1 (January 1965), p. 124. Reprinted in *The Edge of the Chair*, ed, Joan Kahn (New York, 1967), pp. 120-3 , and in: *The Tea Party and Other Plays*, (London: Methuen, 1974), pp. 116-121. 'The Black and White', *Transatlantic Review*, 21, pp. 51-2.

ESSAYS AND SPEECHES

'Art as Therapy, Hobby, or Experience', in *Essays in Honour of William Gallacher* (Berlin, 1966), pp. 234-6.

'Beckett', in *Beckett at Sixty: a Festschrift*, ed. J. Calder (London, 1967), p. 86.

'Blood sports', *Hackney Downs School Magazine*, 163 (Autumn 1947), pp. 23-4.

'James Joyce', *Hackney Downs School Magazine*, 160 (Christmas 1946), pp. 32-3.

'The Knight Has Been Unruly: Memories of Sir Donald Wolfit', *The Listener*, LXXIX, 2038 (18 April 1968), p. 501.

'Mac', *Harper's Bazaar*, 102 (November 1968), pp. 234-5. Also in *Good Talk 2: an Anthology from BBC Radio*, ed. Derwent May (1969); and separately published as *Mac* (London: Pendragon Press, 1968).

'Memories of Cricket', *Daily Telegraph Magazine*, 16 May 1969, pp. 25-6.

'Mr. Losey's Screenplays', *The Times* (19 October, 1972), p. 17.

'Pinter on Pinter', Cinebill, 1, 2 (October, 1973), repr. from *Theatre Quarterly*.

'Pinter on Beckett', *New Theatre Magazine*, XI, 3, p. 3.

'Pinter's Reply to Open Letter by Leonard Russell', *The Sunday Times*, 14 August 1960, p. 21.

'Speech: Hamburg 1970', *Theatre Quarterly*, I, 3 (July-September 1971), pp. 3-4.

'Speech: Realism and Post-Realism in the French Cinema', *Hackney Downs School Magazine*, 163 (Autumn 1947), p. 13.

Speech: Supporting the Notion that "In View of its Progress in Last Decade, the Film is More Promising in its Future as an Art than the Theatre', *Hackney Downs School Magazine*, 164 (Spring 1948), p. 12.

'Speech: That a United Europe Would Be the Only Means of Preventing War', *Hackney Downs School Magazine*, 161 (Spring 1947), p. 14.

'Speech: That the War is Inevitable', *Hackney Downs School Magazine*, 163 (Summer 1947), p. 9.

'Vladimir Bukovsky', *The Times* (March 22, 1974), p. 17.

'Writing for Myself', *Twentieth Century*, 169 (February 1961), pp. 172-5.

'Writing for the Theatre', *Evergreen Review*, VIII (August-September 1964), pp. 80-2. Also in *English Dramatic Theories: IV: Twentieth Century*, ed. Paul Goetsch (Tübingen, 1972), pp. 118-24; and in *The New British Drama*, ed. Henry Popkin (New York, 1964), pp. 575-80.

The Critical Response

INTERVIEWS

Anon. 'Mr. Harold Pinter — Avant-Garde Playwright and Intimate Revue', *The Times* (16 November, 1959), p. 4.

'The Art of the Theatre III', *The Paris Review*, 39 (Fall 1966), pp. 13-37.

'Critic at Large, Interview with H. Tennyson', B.B.C. General Overseas Service (7 August, 1960).

'Dialogue for Three', *Stand*, VI (1963/64), pp. 4-5.

'Filming *The Caretaker:* Harold Pinter and Clive Donner interviewed by Kenneth Lavander', *Transatlantic Review,* 13 (Summer 1963), pp. 17 pp. 17-26. Also in *Behind the Scenes,* ed. Joseph McCrindle (London, 1971), pp. 211-22.

Gussow, M., 'A Conversation with Harold Pinter', *New York Times Magazine,* 5 December 1971, pp. 42-3, 126-36.

'Harold Pinter: an Interview with L.M. Bensky'. Originally published as 'The Art of the Theatre, III', *Paris Review*, 39 (Fall 1966), pp. 13-37. Reprinted in *Theatre at Work,* ed. Charles Marowitz and Simon Trussler (London, 1967), pp. 96-109; in *The Paris Review Interviews: Third Series* (London, 1968), pp. 347-368; in *The Playwright Speaks,* ed. W. Wager (London, 1969), pp. 136-149; in *Writers at Work: Interviews from Paris Review,* ed. Kay Dick (Harmondsworth, 1972), pp. 296-314; and in *Pinter: a Collection of Critical Essays,* ed. Arthur Ganz (Englewood Cliffs, N.J., 1972), pp. 19-33.

'Harold Pinter Replies: Pinter Interviewed by Harry Thompson', *New Theatre Magazine,* XI, 2 (January, 1961), pp. 8-10.

'Harold Pinter Talks to Michael Dean', *The Listener,* LXXXI, 2084 (March, 1969), p. 312.

'In an Empty Bandstand — Harold Pinter in Conversation with Joan Bakewell', *The Listener,* LXXXII, 2119 (November 1969), pp. 630-63.

'Interview with Joan Bakewell', B.B.C. II TV (11 September, 1969).

'Interview with Michael Dean', B.B.C. II TV ('Late Night Up').

'Interview with John Kershaw', I.T.V. (1964).

'Interview with Paul Mayersberg and Laurence Kitchin', B.B.C. III (19 October, 1963), ('New Comment').

'Interview with Harold Pinter', *Daily Mirror* (26 March, 1965).

'Interview with Harold Pinter', *New York Times* (10 September, 1967), sec. 2, p. 3.

'Interview with Harold Pinter', *New York Times* (27 October, 1968), sec. 2, p. 3.

'Interview with John Sherwood', B.B.C. European Service (3 March, 1960), ('The Rising Generation').

'Interview with Kenneth Tynan', B.B.C. Home Service (28 October, 1960), 19 August 1960, ('People Today').

'Interview with Owen Webster', B.B.C. (2 June, 1960).

'Interview with Hew Wheldon', B.B.C. TV (5 June, 1960), ('Monitor').

'Interview with Carl Wildman and Donald McWhinnie', B.B.C. III (7 March, 1961), ('Talking of Theatre').

'In Search of Harold Pinter: Interview with Kathleen Tynan', *Evening Standard*, Part I (25 April, 1968), Part II (26 April, 1968).

Packard, William. 'An Interview with Harold Pinter', *First Stage*, VI, 2 (Summer, 1967), p. 82.

'Pinter Between the Lines', *The Sunday Times* (4 March, 1962), p. 25.

'Pinter on the Screen', Picture Parade 25, B.B.C. Transcription Service.

'Pinter People', produced for *NBC Experiment*.

'Pinter: Violence Is Natural. Interview with Harold Pinter', *New York Times* (1 January, 1967), sec. 2, p. 1.

'Trying to Pin Down Pinter: Interview with Marshall Pugh', *Daily Mail* (7 March, 1964).

'Two People in a Room', *The New Yorker* (25 February, 1967), pp. 34-36.

'Über das Schreiben von Theaterstücken', *Die Neue Rundschau*, Jg. 74 (1963), pp. 503-509, translation of 'Between the Lines'.

BIBLIOGRAPHIES AND CHECKLISTS

Adelman, Irving, and Rita Dworkin, 'Harold Pinter', in *Modern Drama* (Metuchen, N.J., 1967), pp. 241-2

Gale, Steven H., 'Harold Pinter: an Annotated Bibliography, 1957-1971', *Bulletin of Bibliography*, XXIX, 2 (April-June 1972), pp. 45-56.

Gordon, Lois G., 'Pigeonholing Pinter: a Bibliography', *Theatre Documentation*, I, 1 (Fall 1968), pp. 3-20.

Majstrak, Manfred, and Hans Rossman, 'Harold Pinter', in *Bibliographie der Interpretationen: Englisch* (Dortmund, 1972), pp. 117-20.

Palmer, David S., 'A Harold Pinter Checklist', *Twentieth Century Literature*, XVI, 4 (October 1970), pp. 287-96.

Schroll, Herman T., *Harold Pinter: a Study of His Reputation, 1958-1969, and a Checklist* (Metuchen, N.J., 1971).

Stoll, Karl-Heinz. *The New British Drama: A Bibliography with Particular Reference to Arden, Bond, Osborne, Pinter, Wesker* (Bern, Frankfurt: Lang, 1975), pp. 12-14, 20-21; 39-51.

BIOGRAPHICAL MATERIAL

'Caretaker's Caretaker', *Time*, LXXVIII, 19 (10 November, 1961), p. 76.

'Harold Pinter', in *Current Biography*, ed. Charles Moritz (New York, 1963), pp. 326-9.

Jones, Mervyn, 'Harold Pinter' *Time Out*, 10-17 June 1971 pp. 35-37.

Marowitz, Charles, 'A Biographical Article on Harold Pinter', *New York Times*, 1 October 1967, sec.2, p. 36.

'People Are Talking About . . . . ', *Vogue*, 139 (15 January 1962), pp. 38-9.

'Vivien Merchant and Harold Pinter: a Kitchen Set for a Working Life', *Vogue*, (December 1967), pp. 104-5.

GENERAL CRITICAL MATERIAL

Aaron, Jules L., 'The Audience in the Mirror: the Role of Game Ritual In Contemporary Theatre', *Dissertation Abstracts International*, 31: 5563A.

Abirached, Robert, 'Le Jeune Theatre Anglais', *Nouvelle Revue Française*, XXIX, 170 (February 1967) pp. 314-21.

Ahrens, Rüdiger, 'Das moderne englische Drama: Möglichkeiten der Behandlung im Unterricht der gymnasialen Oberstufe', *Der fremdsprachliche Unterricht*, IV, 13 (February 1970), pp. 15-28.

Allgaier, Dieter, *An Interpretation of Harold Pinter's 'The Caretaker'* (Frankfurt/A,M,, Berlin, Munchen, 1971).

Allgaier, Dieter. *Die Dramen Harold Pinters: eine Untersuchung von Inhalt und Form*, (Dissertation, Frankfurt, 1968).

Allgaier, Dieter, 'Harold Pinter', *Praxis des neusprachlichen Unterrichts*, XV (1968), pp. 403-7.

Allgaier, Dieter, 'Harold Pinters *The Caretaker* als Lese-und Diskussionsstoff in der gymnasialen Oberstufe', *Die Neueren Sprachen*, 11 (November 1970), pp. 556-66.

Allison, Ralph, and Charles Wellborn, 'Rhapsody in an Anechoic Chamber: Pinter's *Landscape, Educational Theatre Journal*, XXV (May 1973), pp. 215-25.

Amend, Victor E., 'Harold Pinter: Some Credits and Some Debits', *Modern Drama*, X, 2 (September 1967), pp; 165-74.

Angus, William, 'Modern Theatre Reflects the Times', *Queen's Quarterly*, LXX, 2 (Summer 1963), pp. 255-63.

Aragones, Juan Emilio, 'Dos hermeticas piezas breves de Harold Pinter', *La Estafeta Literaria*, 31 (February 1967).

Arden, John, 'A Thoroughly Romantic View', *London Magazine*, VII (1960), pp. 11-15.

Arden, John, *'The Caretaker'*, *New Theatre Magazine*, I, 4 (July 1960), pp. 29-30.

Armstrong, William A., ed., *Experimental Drama* (London, 1963).

Armstrong, William A., 'Tradition and Innovation in the London Theatre, 1960-1961', *Modern Drama*, IV, 2 (September 1961), pp. 184-95.

Aronson, Steven M. L., 'Pinter's 'Family' and Blood Knowledge', in *A Casebook on Harold Pinter's* 'The Homecoming' (New York, 1971), pp. 67-86.

Ashworth, Arthur, 'New Theatre: Ionesco, Beckett, Pinter', *Southerly*, XXII, 3, (1962), pp. 145-54.

Baker, William, and Stephen E. Tabachnick, *Harold Pinter* (Edinburgh, 1973).

"Bank Governor Made Privy Councillor", *The Times* (11 June, 1966), pp. 1, 14.

Becherman, Bernard, *Dynamics of Drama: Theory and Method of Analysis* (New York, 1970), pp. 238-9.

Beckmann, Heinz, 'Harold Pinter', *Zeitwende*, 31 (1960), pp.858-9.

Berkowitz, Gerald M., *The Question of Identity in the Plays of Harold Pinter*, Thesis, Columbia University, 1965.

Bernhard, F.J., 'Beyond Realism: the Plays of Harold Pinter', *Modern Drama*, VIII, 2 (September 1965), pp. 185-91.

Bernhard, F.J., 'English Theatre 1963: in the Wake of the New Wave', *Books Abroad*, 38, pp. 143-144.

Bigsby, C.W.E., 'Pinter', in *Contemporary Dramatists*, ed. James Vinson (London, 1973), pp; 608-13.

Billington, Michael, 'Our Theatre in the Sixties', in *Theatre 71*, ed. Sheridan Morley (London, 1971), pp. 208-33.

Black, Susan M., 'Play Reviews', *Theatre Arts*, XLV, 12 (December 1961), pp. 12-13.

Blau, Herbert, 'Politics and the Theatre', *Wascana Review*, II, 2 (1967) pp. 5-23.

Blau, Herbert, *The Impossible Theatre: a Manifesto* (New York, 1964), pp. 254-6.

Bleich, David, 'Emotional Origin of Literary Meaning', *College English*, XXXI, 1 (October 1969), pp. 30-40.

Boulton, James T., 'Harold Pinter: *The Caretaker* and Other Plays', *Modern Drama*, VI, 2 (September 1963), pp. 131-40. Reprinted in

Pinter: a Collection of Critical Essays, ed. A. Ganz (Englewood Cliffs, N.J., 1972), pp. 93-104.

Bovie, Palmer, 'Seduction: the Amphitryon Theme from Plautus to Pinter', *Minnesota Review*, VII, 3-4 (1967), pp. 304-13.

Bowen, John, 'Accepting the Illusion', *Twentieth Century*, CLXIX (February 1961), pp. 152-65.

Bowen, John, 'Changing Fashions in the English Theatre', *The Listener*, LX (1958), p. 269.

Boyum, Joy Gould, and Adrienne Scott, eds., *Film as Film: Critical Responses to Film Art* (Boston, 1971), pp. 26-44.

Bradbrook, M.C., *English Dramatic Form: a History of its Development* (London, 1965), pp. 188-90.

Bray, J.J., 'The Ham Funeral', *Meanjin*, 21 (March 1962), pp. 32-4.

Bredella, Lothar, 'Die Intention und Wirkung literarischer Texte: Arnold Weskers *Chips With Everything* und Harold Pinters *The Birthday Party*', *Der fremdsprachliche Unterricht*, Jg. 7,25 (February 1073), pp. 34-49.

Brine, Adrian, 'Mac Davies is No Clochard', *Drama*, 61 (Summer 1961), pp. 35-7.

'British Theatre, 1956-1966', *Tulane Drama Review*, XI, 2 (Winter 1966), pp. 29-206.

Brook, Peter, Peter Hall, Michel St. Denis, and Peter Shaffer, 'Artaud for Artaud's Sake', *Encore*, XI, 3 (May–June 1964), pp.20-31.

Brooke, Nicholas, 'The Characters of Drama', *Critical Quarterly*, VI (1964), pp. 72-82.

Brown, John Russell, 'Dialogue in Pinter and Others', *Critical Quarterly*, VII (Autumn 1965), pp. 223-43. Reprinted in *Modern British Dramatists*, ed. J.R. Brown (Englewood Cliffs, N.J., 1968), pp. 122-44.

Brown, John Russell, 'Mr. Pinter's Shakespeare', *Critical Quarterly*, V, 3 (Autumn 1963), pp. 251-65. Reprinted in *Essays on Modern Drama* (Boston, 1964), pp. 352-66.

Brown, John Russell, *Theatre Language: a Study of Arden, Osborne, Pinter, and Wesker* (London, 1972), pp. 15-117.

Browne, E. Martin, 'A Look Round the English Theatre 1961', *Drama Survey*, 1, (1961), pp. 227-31.

Brulez, Raymond, 'Nieuwe dramatik?', *Nieuwe Vlaams Tijdschrift*, XVIII (1965), pp. 835-6.

Brustein, Robert, 'The English Stage', *Tulane Drama Review*, X (Spring 1966), pp127-33.

Brustein, Robert, *Seasons of Discontent: Dramatic Opinions, 1959-1965* (New York, 1965).

Brustein, Robert, *The Theatre of Revolt* (London, 1965).

Brustein, Robert, *The Third Theatre* (London, 1967).

Bryden, Ronald, 'Pinter', *The Observer*, (19 February 1967), p.11.

Bryden, Ronald, *The Unfinished Hero* (London, 1969).

Burkman, Katherine H., 'Pinter's *A Slight Ache* as Ritual', *Modern Drama*, XI (December, 1968), pp. 326-35.

Burkman, Katherine. *The Dramatic World of Harold Pinter. Its Basis in Ritual* (Columbus, 1971).

Busch, Lloyd, 'The Plot-Within-the-Plot: Harold Pinter's *The Caretaker*', paper given at the S.A.A. Convention, Los Angeles, 8 December 1967.

Cain, Cindy S.A.M., 'Structure in the One-Act Play', *Modern Drama*, XII (1969-70), pp. 390-98.

Callen, A., 'Comedy and Passion in the Plays of Harold Pinter', *Forum of Modern Language Studies*, IV, 3 (July 1968), pp. 299-305.

Callen, A., 'Stoppard's Godot: Some French Influences on Post-War English Drama', *New Theatre Magazine*, X, 1, pp. 22-30.

Canady, Nicholas, Jr., 'Harold Pinter's *Tea Party*', *Studies in Short Fiction*, VI (Fall 1969), pp. 580-85.

Capone, Giovanna, *Drammi per voci: Dylan Thomas, Samuel Beckett, Harold Pinter* (Bologna, 1967).

Carat, J., 'Harold Pinter and W. Gombrowicz', *Preuves*, 117 (November 1965), pp. 75-7.

Carpenter, Charles A., 'The Absurdity of Dread: Pinter's *The Dumb Waiter*', *Modern Drama*, XVI, 3-4 (December 1973), pp. 279-85.

Case, L.L., 'A Parody on Harold Pinter's Style of Drama', *New York Times*, 16 May 1965, p. 6.

Chiari, Joseph, *Landmarks of Contemporary Drama* (London, 1965).

'CBS Says That it Wants Pinter and Vidal Scripts', *New York Times*, 4 November 1967, p. 66.

Clurman, Harold, *The Naked Image: Observations on the Modern Theatre* (New York, 1966).

Cohen, Mark, 'The Plays of Harold Pinter', *Jewish Quarterly*, VIII, 3 (Summer 1961), pp. 21-2.

Cohen, Marshall, 'Theatre 67', *Partisan Review*, XXXIV, 3 (Summer 1967), pp. 436-44.

Cohn, Ruby, *Currents in Contemporary Drama* (Bloomington, 1969).

Cohn, Ruby, 'Latter Day Pinter', *Drama Survey*, III (February 1964), pp. 367-77.

Cohn, Ruby, 'The Absurdly Absurd: Avatars of Godot', *Contemporary Literature Studies*, II, 3 (1965), pp. 233-40.

Cohn, Ruby, 'The World of Harold Pinter', *Tulane Drama Review,* VI (March 1962), pp. 55-68. Reprinted in *Pinter: a Collection of Critical Essays,* ed. A. Ganz (Englewood Cliffs, N.J., 1972), pp. 78-92.

Conlon, Partick O., 'Social Documentary in Contemporary Great Britain, as Reflected in the Plays of John Osborne, Harold Pinter, and Arnold Wesker', *Dissertation Abstracts,* 29: 3713A-14A.

Cook, David, 'Of the Strong Breed', *Transition,* III, 13 (March–April 1964), pp. 38-40.

Cook, David, and Harold F. Brooks, 'A Room with Three Views: Harold Pinter's *The Caretaker',* *Komos,* 1 (1967), pp. 62-9.

Corrie, Tim, *'The Homecoming', New Theatre Magazine,* VI, 2 (1965), pp. 31-2.

Cowan, Margaret, 'The World of Harold Pinter', *The Stage,* 5 May 1960, p. 19.

Craig, H.A.L., 'Poetry in the Theatre', *New Statesman,* LX (12 November 1960), pp. 734, 736.

Crinkley, Richmond, 'The Development of Edward Albee', *National Review,* XXIII, 21, (1 June 1971), pp. 602-4.

Crist, Judith, 'A Mystery: Pinter on Pinter', *Look,* 24 December 1968, pp. 77-80.

Crist, Judith, 'The Agony Beneath the Skin Revealed with Surgical Skill', in *Film as Film: Critical Responses to Film Art,* **ed.,** J.G. Boyum and A. Scott (Boston, 1971), pp. 29-31.

Croyden, Margaret, 'Pinter's Hideous Comedy', in *A Casebook on Harold Pinter's The Homecoming,* ed. John Lahr (New York, 1971), pp. 45-56.

'Cues', *Plays and Players,* XXI, 1 (October 1973), p. 17.

Curley, Daniel, 'A Night in the Fun House', *Pinter's Optics,* Midwest Monograph Series I, 1 (September 1967), pp. 1-2.

Davison, Peter, 'Contemporary Drama and Popular Dramatic Forms', in *Aspects of Drama and the Theatre,* ed. R.N. Coe et al. (Sydney, 1965), pp. 143-197.

Dawick, John, 'Punctuation and Patterning in *The Homecoming',* *Modern Drama,* XIV, 1 (May 1971), pp. 37-46.

Dennis, Nigel, 'Pintermania', *New York Review of Books,* 17 December 1970, pp. 21-2.

Dias, Earl J., 'The Enigmatic World of Harold Pinter', *Drama Critique,* XI, 3 (Fall 1968), pp. 119-24.

Dick Kay, 'Pinter and the Fearful Matter', *Texas Quarterly,* VI, 3 (Autumn 1961), pp. 257 -65.

Dillon, Percy, C., 'The Characteristics of the French Theatre of the Absurd in the Plays of Edward Albee and Harold Pinter', *Dissertation Abstracts*, 29: 257A-58A.

Donoghue, Denis, 'London Letter: Moral West End',*Hudson Review*, XIV (Spring 1961), pp.93-103.

Donoghue, Denis, 'The Human Image in Modern Drama', *Lugano Review*, I, 3-4 (1965), pp. 155-68.

Douglas, Reid, 'The Failure of English Realism', *Tulane Drama Review*, VII, 2 (Winter 1962), pp. 180-3.

Downer, Alan S., 'Experience of Heroes', *Quarterly Journal of Speech*, XLVIII, 3 (October 1962), pp. 261-70.

Downer, Alan S., 'Old, New Borrowed and (a Trifle) Blue: Notes on the New York Theatre, 1967-1968', *Quarterly Journal of Speech*, LIV, 3 (October 1968), pp. 199-211.

Downer, Alan S., 'The Doctor's Dilemma: Notes on the New York Theatre', *Quarterly Journal of Speech*, LIII, 3 (October 1967), pp. 213-23.

Drake, Carol Dixon, *Harold Pinter and the Problem of Verification*, Thesis, University of South Carolina, 1964.

Drescher, Horst W., 'Die englische Literatur' in *Moderne Weltliteratur: die Gegenwartsliteratur Europas und Amerikas*, ed. Gero von Wilpert and Ivar Ivask (Stuttgart, 1972), pp. 323-6.

Drescher, Horst W. "Einleitung", in *Englische Literatur in Einzeldarstellungen* (Stuttgart, 1970), pp. 17f.

Duberman, Martin, 'Theatre 69', *Partisan Review*, 3 (1969), pp. 483-500.

Dukore, Bernard, 'The Theatre of Harold Pinter', *Tulane Drama Review*, VI, 3 (March 1962), pp. 43-54.

Dukore, Bernard, 'A Woman's Place', *Quarterly Journal of Speech*, LII, 3 (October 1966), pp. 237-41. Reprinted in *A Casebook on Harold Pinter's The Homecoming*, ed. John Lahr (New York, 1971), pp. 109-16.

Dukore, Bernard, *Encyclopedia of World Drama*, vol. III (New York, 1972), pp. 425-29.

Edwards, Sydney, 'Dark New Adventures in Pinterland', *Evening Standard* 7 May 1971, pp. 24-5.

Edwards, Sydney, 'Four Boundaries for Mr. Pinter', *Evening Standard*, 18 July 1971, p. 21.

Edwards, Sydney, 'Pinter, The Crisis Over', *Evening Standard*, 21 August 1970, pp. 16-17.

Eigo, James, 'Pinter's *Landscape*', *Modern Drama*, XVI, 2 (September 1973), pp. 179-83.

Elsom, John, 'The End of the Absurd', *London Magazine*, IV, 3 (June 1964), pp. 62-6.

Ekbom, Torsten, 'Pa jakt efter en identitet: Harold Pinter och den absurda traditionen', *Bonniers Litterara Magasin*, 31, (1962), pp. 809-14.

Engler, Balz, 'Shakespeare und das moderne Theater:eine Konfrontation auf der Buhne', in *Deutsche Shakespeare Gesellschaft West, Jahrbuch 1971*, ed. Heuer, Hermann (Heidelburg, 1971), pp. 18-22.

Englisches Theater unserer Zeit, with an introduction by Friedrich Luft (Reinbeck, 1961).

Esslin, Martin, 'Brecht, the Absurd, and the Future', *Tulane Drama Review,* VII, 4 (Summer 1963), pp. 43-54.

Esslin, Martin. *Brief Chronicles: Essays on the Modern Theatre* (London, 1970).

Esslin, Martin, 'Der Commonsense des Nonsense', in *Sinn oder Unsinn: Theater unserer Zeit,* Vol. III (Stuttgart, Basel, 1962).

Esslin, Martin, 'Godot and his Children', in *Experimental Drama,* ed. W.A. Armstrong (London, 1963), pp. 128-46. Reprinted in *Modern British Dramatists,* ed. J.R. Brown (Englewood Cliffs, N.J., 1968), pp. 58-70.

Esslin, Martin, 'Harold Pinter: un dramaturgue anglais de l'absurde', *Preuves,* 151 (September 1963), pp. 45-54.

Esslin, Martin. *Harold Pinter ou le double jeu du langage,* /Translation of *The Peopled Wound/* (Paris, 1972).

Esslin, Martin, 'Language and Silence' in *Pinter: A Collection of Critical Essays* ed. A. Ganz (Englewood Cliffs, N.J., 1972), pp. 34-59.

Esslin, Martin, 'New Form in the Theatre' in *Reflections: Essays on Modern Theatre* (Garden City, New York, 1969), pp. 3-10.

Esslin, Martin. *Pinter,* Friedrichs Dramatiker, Vol. XXXVIII (Velber, 1967), reprint.

Esslin, Martin, 'Pinter and the Absurd', *Twentieth Century,* CLXIX, 1008 (February 1961), pp. 176-185.

Esslin, Martin, *Pinter: a Study of his Plays* (London, 1973). Earlier edition published under the title *The Peopled Wound: the Plays of Harold Pinter* (London, 1970).

Esslin, Martin, 'Pinter Translated: on International Non-Communication', *Encounter,* XXX, 3 (March 1968), pp. 45-7, and in M. Esslin, *Brief Chronicles,* pp. 190-195.

Esslin, Martin, 'The Absurdity of the Absurd', *Kenyon Review,* XXII (Autumn 1960), pp. 670-3.

Esslin, Martin, *'The Homecoming:* an Interpretation', in *A Casebook* on *Harold Pinter's The Homecoming,* ed. John Lahr (New York, 1971), pp. 1-8.

Esslin, Martin *The Theatre of the Absurd,* revised updated edition (London, 1974).

Esslin, Martin. 'The Theatre of the Absurd Reconsidered', in: M. Esslin *Reflections on Modern Theatre,* pp. 183-191, and in: M. Esslin *Brief Chronicles . . .* , pp. 219-227.

Esslin, Martin, 'Violence in Drama', *Encounter,* XI, 3 (May—June 1964), pp. 6-15.

Evans, Gareth Lloyd, 'Pinter's Black Magic', *The Guardian,* 30 September 1965, p. 8; also in *The Curtain Rises,* Leslie Frenzin coup, by Rich Richards, 1966, pp. 68-72.

Farrington, Conor, 'The Language of Drama', *Tulane Drama Review,* V, gen. (December 1960), pp. 65-72.

Feldmann, Heinz, 'Harold Pinter', in *Englische Literatur der Gegenwart in Einzeldarstellungen,* ed. H.W. Drescher (Stuttgart, 1970), pp. 431-57.

Feynman, Alberta E., 'The Fetal Quality of 'Character' in Plays of the Absurd', *Modern Drama,* IX (May 1966), pp. 18-25.

Fields, Suzanne, 'Levels of Meaning in Structural Patterns of Allegory and Realism in Selected Plays of Harold Pinter', *Dissertation Abstracts International,* 32: 2087A-88A.

Fischer, Peter, 'Versuch uber das scheinbar absurde Theater', *Merkur,* XIX, 2 (1965), pp. 151-63.

Fitzgerald, Marion, 'Playwriting is Agony, Says Hugh Leonard', *Irish Digest,* LXXIX, 3 (January 1964), pp. 34-6.

Fjelde, Rolf, 'Plotting Pinter's Progress', in *A Casebook on Harold Pinter's The Homecoming,* ed. John Lahr (New York, 1971), pp. 87-107.

Fletcher, John, 'Harold Pinter, Rolland Dubillard, and Eugene Ionesco', *Caliban,* III, 2 (1967), pp. 149-52.

Franzblau, Abraham, 'A Psychiatrist Looks at *The Homecoming,*' *Saturday Review,* 8 April 1967, p. 58.

Fraser, G.S., *The Modern Writer and His World* (Harmondsworth, 1970), pp. 238-43.

Free, William J., 'Treatment of Character in Harold Pinter's *The Homecoming',* *South Atlantic Bulletin,* XXXIV, 4 (November 1969), pp. 1-5.

Freedman, Morris *Essays on the Modern Drama* (Boston, 1964).

Freedman, Morris, *The Moral Impulse: Modern Drama from Ibsen to the Present* (Carbondale, Ill., 1967), pp. 124-6.

Fricker, Robert, *Das moderne englische Drama* (Göttingen, 1974), pp. 166-170, 179-184.

Frisch, Jack Eugene, 'Ironic Theatre: Techniques of Irony in the Plays of Harold Pinter, Samuel Beckett, Eugene Ionesco, and Jean Genet', *Dissertation Abstracts,* 25: 6114A-5A.

'From Page to Screen: Harold Pinter, *Five Screenplays', Times Literary Supplement,* 361 6 (18 June, 1971), p. 695.

Gale, John, 'Taking Pains With Pinter', *The Observer,* 10 June 1962, p. 19.

Gale, Steven H., *Harold Pinter's* The Birthday Party *and Other Works,* Monarch Notes No. 910 (New York, 1972).

Gale, Steven H., *Harold Pinter's* The Homecoming *and Other Works,* Monarch Notes No. 906 (New York 1971).

Gale, Steven H., 'Thematic Change in the Stage Plays of Harold Pinter, 1957-1967', *Dissertation Abstracts International,* 31: 3546A.

Gallagher, Kent, 'Harold Pinter's Dramaturgy', *Quarterly Journal of Speech,* LII, 3 (October 1966), pp. 242-8.

Ganz, Arthur, 'A Clue to the Pinter Puzzle: the Triple Self in *The Homecoming', Educational Theatre Journal,* XXI (May 1969), pp. 180-7.

Ganz, Arthur, 'Mixing Memory and Desire: Pinter's Vision in *Landscape, Silence,* and *Old Times',* in *Pinter: a Collection of Critical Essays,* ed. A. Ganz (Englewood Cliffs, N.J., 1972), pp. 161-78.

Ganz, Arthur, ed., *Pinter: a Collection of Critical Essays* (Englewood Cliffs, N.J., 1972).

Gascoigne, Bamber, *Twentieth Century Drama* (London, 1962).

Gassner, John, 'Foray into the Absurd', in *Dramatic Soundings* (New York, 1969), pp. 503-7.

Gassner, John, 'Osborne and Pinter', in *The World of Contemporary Drama* (New York, 1965), pp. 21-3.

Geduld, Harry M., 'The Trapped Heroes of Harold Pinter', *Humanist,* XXVIII (March—April 1968), pp. 24ff.

Gianetti, Louis D., 'The Drama of the Welfare State', *Dissertation Abstracts,* 28:229A-230A.

Gillen, Francis, 'Apart from the Known and the Unknown: the Unreconciled Worlds of Pinter's Characters', *Arizona Quarterly,* XXVI, pp. 17-24.

Gilman, Richard, 'The Pinter Puzzle', *New York Times,* 22 January 1967, sec. 2, p. 1.

Glover, William, 'Pinter's Plays Reflect His Cool', *Los Angeles Times,* 14 May 1967.

Goetsch, Paul 'Das englische Drama seit Shaw', in *Das englische Drama.* ed. Josefa Nunning (Darmstadt, 1973), pp. 403-507.

Goetsch, Paul, *English Dramatic Theories, IV: Twentieth Century* (Tubingen, 1972), pp. 118-24.

Goetsch, Paul, 'Harold Pinter: *Old Times',* in *Das englische Drama der*

Gegenwart, ed. H. Oppel (Berlin, 1976).

Goldstone, Herbert, 'Not So Puzzling Pinter: *The Homecoming',
Theatre Annual,* 25 (1969), pp. 20-7.

Goodman, Florence J., 'Pinter's *The Caretaker:* the Lower Depths
Descended', *Midwest Quarterly,* V, 2 (Winter 1964), pp. 117-26.

Gordon, Lois G., 'Harold Pinter: Past and Present', *Kansas Quarterly,*
III, 2 (1971), pp. 89-99.

Gordon, Lois G., *Stratagems to Uncover Nakedness* (Columbia, 1969).

Gray, Wallace, 'The Use of Incongruity', *Educational Theatre Journal,*
XV, 4 (December 1963), pp. 343-7.

Gross, John, 'Amazing Reductions', *Encounter,* (September 1964),
pp.50-2.

Guthke, Karl S., 'Die metaphysische Farce in Theater der Gegenwart',
Deutsche Shakespeare Gesellschaft West Jahrbuch, 1970 (Heidelburg,
1970), pp. 49-76.

Habicht, Werner. 'Der Dialog und das Schweigen im Theater
des Absurden' , *Die Neueren Sprache,* 2 (1967), pp. 53-66.

Habicht, Werner, 'Theater der Sprache', *Die Neueren Sprachen,* 7
(July 1963), pp. 302-13.

Hafley, James, 'The Human Image in Contemporary Art', *Kerygma,* 3
(Summer 1963), pp. 23-4.

Hall, Peter, 'Directing Pinter', *Theatre Quarterly,* IV, 16
(November 1974-January 1975), pp. 4-17.

Hall, Peter, 'Is the Beginning the Word?', *Theatre Quarterly* II, 7
(July-September 1972), pp. 5-11.

Hall, Rodney, 'Theatre in London', *Westerly,* 3 (October 1964,
pp. 57-60.

Hall, Stuart, 'Home Sweet Home', *Encore,* XII, 4 (July-August 1965),
pp. 30-4.

Halton, Kathleen, 'Pinter: Funny and Moving and Frightening', *Vogue,*
150 (1 October 1967), pp. 194-5.

Hare, Carl, 'Creativity and Commitment in the Contemporary British
Theatre', *Humanities Association Bulletin,* XVI, 1 (Spring 1965),
pp. 21-8.

Hasler, Jorg, 'Bühnenanweisung und Spiegeltechnik bei Shakespeare
und im modernen Drama', *Deutsche Shakespeare Gesellschaft West
Jahrbuch, 1970* (Heidelburg, 1970), pp. 99-117.

Hayman, Ronald, *Harold Pinter* (London 1970). Reprint.

Hayman, Ronald, 'Landscape Without Pictures: Pinter, Beckett, and
Radio', *London Magazine,* VIII, 4 (July 1968), pp. 72-7.

Hays, H.R., 'Transcending Naturalism', *Modern Drama,* V, 1
(May 1962), pp. 27-36.

Heilman, Robert B., *'The Birthday Party* and *The Firebugs'*, in *Sense and Sensibility in Twentieth Century Writing: a Gathering in Memory of William Van O'Connor,* ed. Brom Weber (Carbondale, 1970), pp. 57-74.

Henkle, Roger B., 'From Pooter to Pinter: Domestic Comedy and Vulnerability', *Critical Quarterly,* XVI, 2 (Summer 1974), pp. 174-89.

Hewes, Henry, 'Probing Pinter's Plays', *Saturday Review,* 8 April 1967, pp. 56 ff.

Hilsky, Martin, 'The Two Worlds of Harold Pinter's Plays', in *Prague Studies in English,* ed. Bohumil Trnka and Zdenek Stribrny (Prague, 1968).

Hinchliffe, Arnold P., 'Drama', in *The Twentieth Century Mind, Volume III: 1945-1965,* ed. C.B. Cox and A.E. Dyson (London, 1972), pp. 414-39.

Hinchliffe, Arnold P., *Harold Pinter,* Twayne's English Authors series (New York, 1967).

Hinchliffe, Arnold P., 'Mr Pinter's Belinda', *Modern Drama,* XI (September 1968), pp. 173-9.

Hinchliffe, Arnold P., *The Absurd,* Critical Idiom series (London, 1969).

Hoefer, Jacqueline, 'Pinter and Whiting: Two Attitudes Toward the Alienated Artist', *Modern Drama,* IV, 4 (February 1962), pp. 402-8.

Holland, Julian, 'The No. 296 All-Night Bus to Success', *Evening News,* 14 May 1960.

Hollis, James, *Harold Pinter: the Poetics of Silence* (Carbondale, 1970).

Hortmann, Wilhelm, *Englische Literatur im 20. Jahrhundert* (Bern, 1965), pp. 177-8.

Houghton, Norris, *Drama and Theatre of the Twentieth Century* (New York, 1971).

Hughes, C., 'Pinter is as Pinter Does', *Catholic World,* 210 (December 1969), pp. 124-6.

Hunt, Albert, 'Around Us . . . Things Are There', *Encore,* VIII, 6 (1961), pp. 24-32.

Hunter, C.K., 'English Drama, 1900-1960', in *The Twentieth Century,* Sphere History of Literature in the English Language, Volume VII, ed. B. Bergonzi (London, 1970), pp. 310-333.

Hutchings, Patrick, 'The Humanism of a Dumb Waiter', *Westerly,* 1 (April 1963), pp. 56-63.

Itzin, Catherine, 'The Pinter Enigma', *Theatre Quarterly,* IV, 13 (February–April 1974) p. 95.

Imhof, Rüdiger, *Harold Pinters gestalterische Mittel im Zusammenhang seines dramatischen Gesamtwerkes (1957-73),* Dissertation, Marburg, 1974. published as *Harold Pinter's Dramaturgie* (Bonn, 1976).

Jones, D.A.N., 'Silent Censorship in Britain', *Theatre Quarterly,* I, 1

(January–March 1971), pp. 22-8.

Kalem, T.E. 'The Roomer', *Time*, 12 October 1970, p. 60.

Karrer, Wolfgang, and Eberhard Kreutzer, *Daten der englischen und amerikanischen Literatur von 1890 bis zur Gegenwart* (Munich, 1973), pp. 225, 235, 259.

Kastor, Frank S., 'Pinter and Modern Tragicomedy', *Wichita State University Bulletin: University Studies*, XLVI, 84 (August 1970),pp. 1-13.

Kathane, Eric, 'Pinter et le realisme irreel', *L'Avant-Scene*, 378 (15 April 1967), p. 9.

Kaufman, Michael W., 'Actions That a Man Might Play: Pinter's *The Birthday Party*', *Modern Drama*, XVI, 2 (September 1973), pp. 167-78.

Kaufman, Stanley, 'Stanley Kaufman on Theatre: *Landscape* and *Silence*', *The New Republic*, CLXII, 17 (25 April 1970), p. 20.

Kennedy, A.K., 'Old and New in London Now', *Modern Drama*, XI, 4 (February 1969), pp. 437-46.

Kerr, Walter, *Harold Pinter*, Columbia Essays on Modern Writers (New York, 1967).

Kerr, Walter, '*The Caretaker*', in *The Theatre in Spite of Itself* (New York, 1963), pp. 116-19.

Kerr, Walter, 'The Hey, Wait a Minute Theatre', in *Thirty Plays Hath November* (New York, 1969), pp. 29-41.

Kerr, Walter, 'The Moment of Pinter', in *Thirty Plays Hath November* (New York, 1969). pp. 41-6.

Kerr, Walter, 'The Theatre is the Victim of a Plot', *New York Times*, 25 June 1967, sec. 4, p. 10.

Kershaw, John, 'Harold Pinter, Dramatist' and 'Language and Communication', in *The Present Stage* (London, 1966), pp. 70-8, 79-87.

Kesting, Marianne, 'Harold Pinter', in *Panorama des zeitgenössischen Theaters* (Munich, 1969), pp. 243-8.

Kitchin, Laurence, *Drama in the Sixties: Form and Interpretation* (London, 1966), pp. 45-53.

Kitchin, Laurence, 'Backwards and Forwards', *Twentieth Century*, CLXIX, 1008, pp. 168-9.

Kitchin, Laurence, *Mid-Century Drama* (London, 1960), pp. 119-22.

Kitchin, Laurence, 'Realism in the English Mid-Century Drama', *World Theatre*, XIV, 1 (January–February 1965), pp. 17-26.

Kleinman, Neil, 'Naming of Names', *Pinter's Optics*, Midwest Monographs, I, 1 (September 1967), pp. 4-5.

Klotz, Friedrich, 'Jean Tardieu: Theatre de Chambre', *Der Fremdsprachliche Unterricht*, 4, 13 (February 1970), pp. 69-83.

Klotz, Günther, *Individuum und Gesellschaft im englischen Drama der Gegenwart: Arnold Wesker und Harold Pinter* (Berlin, 1972).

Knight, G. Wilson, 'The Kitchen Sink: on Recent Developments in Drama', *Encounter*, XXI, 6 (December 1963) pp. 48-54.

Kosok, Heinz, 'Das moderne englische Kurzdrama', *Neusprachliche Mitteilungen aus Wissenschaft und Praxis*, 3 (1970), pp. 131-41.

Kunkel, Francis J., 'The Dystopia of Harold Pinter', *Renascence*, XXI (Autumn 1968), pp. 17-20.

Lahr, John, 'An Actor's Approach: an Interview with John Normington', in *A Casebook on Harold Pinter's The Homecoming*, ed. J. Lahr (New York, 1971), pp. 137-50.

Lahr, John, 'An Actor's Approach: an Interview with Paul Roger', in *A Casebook on Harold Pinter's The Homecoming*, ed. J. Lahr (New York, 1971), pp. 151-73.

Lahr, John, ed., *A Casebook on Harold Pinter's The Homecoming* (New York, 1971).

Lahr, John, 'A Designer's Approach: an Interview with John Bury', in *A Casebook on Harold Pinter's The Homecoming*, ed. J. Lahr (New York, 1971), pp. 27-35.

Lahr, John, 'Cracking the Pinter Puzzle', *Evergreen Review*, XV, 86 (January 1971), pp. 74-6.

Lahr, John, 'Harold Pinter', in *On Contemporary Literature* (New York, 1969), pp. 682-9.

Lahr, John, 'The Language of Silence', *Evergreen Review*, XIII, 64 (March 1969), pp. 53-5, 82-90.

Lahr, John, 'Pinter and Chekhov: the Bond of Naturalism', *Tulane Drama Review*, XIII, 2 (Winter 1968), pp. 137-45. Reprinted in *Pinter: a Collection of Critical Essays,* ed. A. Ganz (Englewood Cliffs, N.J., 1972), pp; 60-71.

Lahr, John, 'Pinter's Language', in *A Casebook on Harold Pinter's The Homecoming*, ed. J. Lahr (New York, 1971), pp. 123-36.

Lahr, John, 'Pinter's Room: Who's There?', *Arts Magazine*, March 1967 pp. 21-3.

Lahr, John, 'Pinter the Spaceman', *Evergreen Review*, XII, 5 (June 1968), pp. 49-52, 87-90. Reprinted in *A Casebook on Harold Pinter's The Homecoming*, ed. J. Lahr (New York, 1971), pp. 175-93.

Lambert, J.W. 'Introduction', in *New English Dramatists 3*, ed. Tom Maschler (Harmondsworth, 1961), pp. 7-10.

Lambert, J.W., 'Plays in Performance', *Drama*, 66 (Autumn 1962), pp. 18-25.

Landstone, Charles, 'From John Osborne to Shelagh Delaney', *World Theatre*, 8 (1959), pp. 203-16.

Lane, John Francis, 'No Sex Please, I'm English: John Francis Lane on the Pinter-Visconti Case', *Plays and Players*, XX, 12 (July 1973), pp. 19-21.

Langley, Lee, 'Genius - a Change of Direction', *Daily Telegraph Magazine*, 13 December 1973, pp. 30-36.

Lechler, Hans-Joachim, 'Harold Pinters Sketch *Last to Go*', *Der fremdsprachliche Unterricht*, 4, 13 (February 1970), pp. 29-37.

Leech, Clifford, *The Dramatist's Experience* (London, 1970).

Leech, Clifford, 'Two Romantics: Arnold Wesker and Harold Pinter', in *Contemporary Theatre*, Stratford-upon-Avon Studies, IV (London, 1962), pp. 11-31; also in *Interpretationen X: Englische Literatur* ed. W. Erzgräber (Frankfurt, 1970), pp. 329-52.

Lesser, Simon O., 'Reflections on Pinter's *The Birthday Party*', *Contemporary Literature*, XIII, 1 (1972), pp. 34-43.

Levidova, I., 'A New Hero Appears in the Theatre', *Inostrannaya Literatura*, 1 (January 1962), pp. 201-8.

Lewis, Peter, 'Harold Pinter, Fascinated by Unsatisfactory People', *Time and Tide*, 43 (21 June 1962), pp. 16-17.

Leyburn, Ellen D., 'Comedy and Tragedy Transposed', *Yale Review*, LIII, 4 (Summer 1964), pp. 553-62.

Loney, Glenn M., 'Theatre of the Absurd: Is It Only a Fad?', *Theatre Arts*, XLVI, 11 (November 1962), pp. 20, 22, 24, 66-8.

Lubbren, Rainer, 'Robbe-Grillet, Pinter, und 'Die blaue Villa in Hong-Kong', *Die neue Rundschau*, LXXVIII, 1 (1967), pp. 119-126.

Lumley, Frederick, 'Harold Pinter', in *New Trends in Twentieth Century Drama* (London, 1967), pp. 266-73.

MacNeice, Louis, *Varieties of Parable* (Cambridge, 1965), pp. 121-3.

Malpas, E.R.H., 'A Critical Analysis of the Stage Plays of Harold Pinter', *Dissertation Abstracts*, 27: 1955A.

Mander, Gertrud, 'Die jungen englischen Dramatiker', *Neue deutsche Hefte*, 83, (1961), pp. 104-30.

Mander, Gertrud, 'Wie langweilig is das Ordinare? ', *Theater Heute*, February 1966, pp. 4-5.

Manvell, Roger, 'Pinter Through French Eyes', *Humanist*, 134 (May 1969), pp.142-4.

Manvell, Roger, 'The Decade of Harold Pinter', *Humanist*, 132 (April 1967), pp. 112-15.

Marowitz, Charles, *Confessions of a Counterfeit Critic* (London, 1973), pp. 47-9, 163-5, 184-8.

Marowitz, Charles, 'Heroes and Un-Heroes', *Drama*, 60 (Spring 1961), pp. 39-43.

Marowitz, Charles, 'New Wave in a Dead Sea', *Quarterly Review*, I, 4 (1960), pp. 270-7.

Marowitz, Charles, 'Notes on the Theatre of Cruelty', *Tulane Drama Review*, XI, 2 (Winter 1966).

Marowitz, Charles, 'Pinterism is Maximum Tension Through Minimum Information', *New York Times Magazine*, 1 October 1967, pp. 36-7, 89-90, 92, 94-96.

Marowitz, Charles. 'Theatre Abroad', *Village Voice* (September 1960), (after Gale).

Marowitz, Charles, and Simon Trussler, eds., *Theatre at Work* (London, 1967).

Marshall, Norman. 'The Plays of Rodney Ackland', *London Magazine*, V, 1 (April 1965), pp. 62-67.

Martineau, Stephen, 'Pinter's *Old Times:* the Memory Game,' *Modern Drama*, XVI, 3-4 (December 1973), pp. 287-97.

Mast, Gerald, 'Pinter's Homecoming', *Drama Survey*, VI, 3 (Spring 1968), pp. 266-77.

McCrindle, Joseph, ed., *Behind the Scenes* (London, 1971), pp. 211-22.

McLaughlin, J., 'Harold Pinter and PBL', *America*, 10 February 1968, p. 193.

McWhinnie, Donald, 'Interview by Robert Rubens', *Transatlantic Review*, 12 (Spring 1963), pp. 34-8.

Mennemeier, Franz M., *Das moderne Drama des Auslandes* (Dusseldorf, 1961).

Messenger, Ann P., 'Blindness and the Problem of Identity in Pinter's Plays', *Die Neueren Sprachen*, 8 (August 1972), pp. 481-90.

Methews, Honor, *The Primal Curse* (London, 1967), pp. 22-23, 198-201.

Milberg, Ruth, '1+1=1: Dialogue and Character Splitting in Harold Pinter', *Die Neueren Sprachen*, LXXII (n.s. XXIII), 3 (June 1974), pp. 225-33.

Milne, Tom, 'The Hidden Face of Violence', in *The Encore Reader*, ed. Charles Marowitz, Tom Milne, and Own Hale, (London, 1965), pp. 115-24. Reprinted in *Modern British Dramatists*, ed. J.R. Brown (Englewood Cliffs, N.J., 1968), pp. 38-46.

Minogue, Valerie, 'Taking Care of *The Caretaker*', *Twentieth Century*, 168 (September 1960), pp. 243-8. Reprinted in *Pinter: a Collection of Critical Essays*, ed. A. Ganz (Englewood Cliffs, N.J., 1972), pp. 72-7.

Morris, Kelly, '*The Homecoming*', *Tulane Drama Review*, XI, 2 (Winter 1966), pp. 185-91.

Morrison, Kristin, 'Pinter and the New Irony', *Quarterly Journal of Speech*, LV, 4 (December 1969), pp. 388-93.

Muir, Kenneth, 'Verse and Prose', in *Contemporary Theatre*, ed. J.R. Brown and B. Harris (London, 1962), pp. 97-115.

Murphy, Robert P. 'Non-Verbal Communication and the Overlooked Action in Pinter's *The Caretaker*', *Quarterly Journal of Speech*, LVIII (February 1972), pp. 41-7.

'Named British Order Commander', *New York Times* 11 June 1966, p. 11.

Nelson, Gerald, 'Harold Pinter Goes to the Movies', *Chicago Review*, XIX, 1 (Summer 1966), pp. 33-43.

Nelson, Hugh, '*The Homecoming:* Kith and Kin', in *Modern British Dramatists*, ed. J.R. Brown (Englewood Cliffs, N.J., 1968), pp. 145-63.

'News From the Universities', *The Times*, 8 September 1970, p. 10.

Nicoll, Allardyce, *English Drama: a Modern Viewpoint* (New York, 1968), pp. 140-44.

Nightingale, Benedict, 'Taking Bloody Liberty', *New Statesman*, 18 July 1969, p. 83.

Nollau, Michael, 'Texterfahrung als Selbsterfahrung: die Lekture von Harold Pinters Fernschspiel *The Basement* and seines Vortrages 'Writing for the Theatre' in Klasse 12', *Die Neuren Sprachen*, LXXIII (n.s. XXIII), 6 (December 1974), pp. 495-511.

Nyszkiewicz, Heinz, '*The Dumb Waiter/The Caretaker*', in *Zeitgenossische englische Dichtung*, Bd. III (Frankfurt, 1968), pp. 210-33.

Odajima, Yushi, 'Pinter Notes', *Eigo Seinen* (1969), pp. 416-7.

'Old Times: Colin Blakely Talks to *Plays and Players*', *Plays and Players*, XVIII, 10 (July 1971), pp. 22, 24.

Oliver, William I., 'Between Absurdity and the Playwright', in *Modern Drama: Essays in Criticism*, ed. T. Bogart and W.I. Oliver (New York, 1965), pp. 3-19.

Orley, Ray, 'Pinter and Menace', *Drama Critique*, XI, 3 (Fall 1968) pp. 124-48.

Pallavicini, Roberto, 'Aspetti della dramaturgia contemporanea', *Aut Aut*, 81 (May 1964), pp. 68-73.

Parker, R.B., 'The Theory and the Theatre of the Absurd', *Queen's Quarterly*, LXXIII, 3 (Autumn 1966), pp. 421-41.

Pease, Nicholas B., 'Role, Ritual and Game in the Plays of Harold Pinter', *Dissertation Abstracts International*, 32: 3324A.

Peel, Marie, 'Violence in Literature', *Books and Bookmen* (February 1972), pp. 20-4.

'Personality of the Month', *Plays and Players*, VIII, 6 (March 1961), p. 3.

Pesta, John, 'Pinter's Usurpers', *Drama Sruvey*, VI, 1 (Spring-Summer 1967), pp. 54-63. Reprinted in *Pinter: a Collection of Critical Essays*, ed. A. Ganz (Englewood Cliffs, N.J., 1972), pp. 123-35.

P.H.S., 'Evacuees Look Back', *The Times*, 4 November 1967, p. 8.

P.H.S., 'Shorter Pinter', *The Times*, 11 April 1969, p. 10.

P.H.S., 'The Times Diary', *The Times*, 7 October 1969, p. 8.

Pierce, Roger N., 'Three Plays Analyses', *Dissertation Abstracts International*, 30: 2660A.

'Pinterview', *Newsweek*, 23 July 1962, p. 69.

'Pinter Gets His Eye In', *Evening News*, 10 April 1969, p. 4.

'Pinter Gives Evidence at Trial', *The Times*, 2 September 1967, p. 3.

'Pinter Has a Forthcoming Play', *The Times*, 10 January 1968, p. 8.

'Pinter to Contribute to Book About Evacuated Child', *The Times*, 4 November 1967, p. 8.

'Pinter to Direct *The Man in the Glass Booth*', *The Times*, 1 June 1967, p. 10.

'Pinter Unperturbed', *Daily Mail*, 28 November 1967, p. 4.

'Playwrights in Apartheid Protest', *The Times*, 26 June 1963, p. 12.

Prickett, Stephen, 'Three Modern English Plays', *Philologica Pragensia*, X, 1 (1967), pp. 12-21.

Prideaux, Tom, 'The Adventurous Play: Stranger to Broadway', in *The Discovery of Drama*, ed. Thomas E. Sanders (Glenville, Ill., 1968), pp. 624-7.

'Profile: Playwright on His Own', *The Observer*, 15 September 1963, p. 13.

Richards, Michael, 'Harold Pinter', in *Englische Dichter der Moderne*, ed. R. Suhnel and D. Riesner (Berlin, 1971), pp. 578-87.

Richardson, Jack, 'English Imports on Broadway', *Commentary*, (June 1967), pp. 73-5.

Rickert, Alfred E., 'Perceiving Pinter', *English Record* XXII, 2 (Winter 1971), pp. 30-5.

Robertson, Roderick, 'A Theatre of the Absurd', *Drama Survey*, II,1 (June 1962), pp. 24-43.

Rodger, Ian, 'The Moron as Hero', *Drama*, 59 (Winter 1960), pp. 36-9.

Roll-Hansen, Diderik, 'Harold Pinter og det absurde drama', *Samtiden*, LXXIV (September 1965), pp. 435-40.

Rosador, Kurt Tetzeli von, 'Pinter: *The Homecoming*', in *Das englische Drama*, ed. Dieter Mehl (Dusseldorf, 1970), pp. 319-35.

Rosador, Kurt Tetzeli von, 'Pinter's Dramatic Method: *Kullus, The Examination, The Basement*', *Modern Drama*, XIV, 2 (September 1971), pp. 195-204.

Roy, Emil *British Drama Since Shaw* (Carbondale, 1972), pp. 115-23.

Rubens, Robert, 'Donald McWhinnie', *Transatlantic Review*, (Spring 1963), pp. 34-8.

Ryan, Stephen, 'The London Stage', *America,* CVII, 30 (27 October 1962), pp. 956-8.

Sainer, Arthur, *'A Slight Ache',* in *The Sleepwalker and the Assassin* (New York, 1964), pp. 99-102.

Salem, D., *Harold Pinter dramaturgue de l'ambiguite* (Paris, 1968).

Salem. D., 'Les adaptations cinematographiques de Pinter', *Etudes Anglaises,* XXV, 4 (1972), pp. 493-505.

Sanders, Walter E., 'The English-Speaking Game Drama', *Dissertation Abstracts International,* 30: 5001A-02A.

Schechner, Richard, 'Puzzling Pinter', *Tulane Drama Review,* XI, 2 (Winter 1966), pp. 176-84.

Scheehan, Peter J., 'Theatre of the Absurd: a Child Studies Himself', *English Journal,* LVIII, 4 (April 1969), pp. 561-5.

Schenker, Ueli, 'Versuche zur Ordnung: Harold Pinter und sein *Caretaker',* *Neue Zürcher Zeitung,* 13 April 1969.

Schiff, Ellen F., 'Pancakes and Soap Suds: a Study of Childishness in Pinter's Plays, *Modern Drama,* XVI, 1 (June 1973), pp. 91-101.

Schlegelmilch, Wolfgang, 'Der Raum des Humanen', *Die Neueren Sprachen,* (July 1964), pp. 328-33.

Schrey, Helmut, 'Das zeitgenossiche englische Drama in Schule und Fernsehen', *Der fremdsprachliche Unterricht,* Jg. 4, 13 (February 1970), pp. 2-14.

Schwarze, Hans-Wilhelm, 'Orientierungslosigkeit und Betroffensein: Spielelemente in Harold Pinters *The Birthday Party',* *Literatur in Wissenschaft und Unterricht,* VII, 2 (August 1974), pp. 98-114.

'Shorter Reviews: *The Homecoming',* *Contemporary Review,* CCVIII (February 1966), p. 112.

Simon, John, 'Theatre Chronicle', *Hudson Review* (1961), pp. 586-92.

Singh, Mohindar, 'Harold Pinter: a Reappraisal', *Indian Journal of English Studies,* 10 (1969), pp. 81-95.

Sinko, Gregorz, 'Atari i Modla Anglia', *Dialogue,* LX, 4 (April 1961), pp. 97-9.

Smallwood, Clyde G., 'Harold Pinter', in *Elements of the Existentialist Philosophy in the Theatre of the Absurd* (Dubuque, Iowa, 1966), pp. 140-5.

Smith, Cecil, 'Pinter: the Compulsion of Playwriting', *Los Angeles Times,* 3 December 1967, pp. 1, 19.

Smith, Frederik N., 'Uncertainty in Pinter: *The Dwarfs',* *Theatre Annual,* 26 (1970), pp. 81-96.

Smith, R.D. 'Back to the Text', in *Contemporary Theatre,* ed. J.R. Brown and B. Harris, pp. 117-37

Spanos, William V., 'The Detective and the Boundary: Some Notes on the Postmodern Literary Imagination', *Boundary*, 2 (Fall 1972), pp. 147-68.

Sprague, Claire, 'Possible or Necessary', *New Theatre Magazine*, VIII, 1 (Autumn 1967), pp. 36-7.

States, Bert O., 'Pinter's *Homecoming:* the Shock of Non-Recognition', *Hudson Review* XXI (Autumn 1968), pp. 474-86. Reprinted in *Pinter: a Collection of Critical Essays*, ed. A. Ganz (Englewood Cliffs, N.J., 1972), pp. 147-60.

States, Bert O., 'The Care for Plot in Modern Drama', *Hudson Review*, XX (Spring 1967), pp. 49-61.

Stein, Karen F., 'Metaphysical Silence in Absurd Drama', *Modern Drama*, XIII, 4 (February 1971), pp. 423-31.

Storch, R.F. 'Harold Pinter's Happy Families', *Massachusetts Review*, VIII (Autumn 1967), pp. 703-12. Reprinted in *Pinter: a Collection of Critical Essays*, ed. A. Ganz (Englewood Cliffs, N.J., 1972), pp. 136-46.

Styan, J.L., 'Television Drama', in *Contemporary Theatre*, ed. J.R. Brown and B. Harris, pp. 185-204.

Styan, J.L., *The Drak Comedy: the Development of Modern Tragic Comedy* (Cambridge, 1968), pp. 234-50.

Styan, J.L., 'The Published Plays After 1956:II', *British Book News*, 301 (September 1965), pp. 601-5.

Sykes, Alrene. 'Introduction', in: Harold Pinter, *The Caretaker* (Sydney, 1965).

Sykes, Alrene, *Harold Pinter* (New York; Queensland, 1970).

Sykes, Alrene, 'Harold Pinter's *Dwarfs*', *Komos*, 1 (June 1967), pp. 70-5.

Tabbert, Reinbert, *Harold Pinters Dramen der verlorenen Identität*, Dissertation, Tubingen, 1969.

Tarn, Adam, 'Die Magie des Absurden', *Theater Heute*, 10 (1965), p. 3.

Taylor, John Russell, 'Harold Pinter', in *Anger and After* (London, revised ed., 1969), pp. 323-59.

Taylor, John Russell, 'British Drama of the Fifties', *World Theatre*, II, 3 (Autumn 1962), pp. 241-54.

Taylor, John Russell, *Harold Pinter* (Harlow, 1969).

Taylor, John Russell, 'A Pinter Power Struggle', *Plays and Players*, (August 1965), pp. 34-5.

Taylor, John Russell, 'Pinter's Game of Happy Families', in *A Casebook on Harold Pinter's The Homecoming*, ed. J. Lahr (New York, 1971), pp. 57-65.

Taylor, John Russell, 'Pinter Pointers', *Times Literary Supplement*, 3305 (1 July 1965), p. 552.

Taylor, John Russell. 'A Room and Some Views; Harold Pinter', in:

A. Ganz (ed.), *Pinter: A Collection of Critical Essays,* pp. 105-122.

Taylor, John Russell, *The Rise and the Fall of the Well-Made Play,* (New York, 1967), pp. 162-64.

Taylor, John Russell, 'What's Happened to the New Dramatists?', *Plays and Players* XI, 11 (August 1964), pp. 8-9.

Theater heute - Theater 63: Chronik und Bilanz eines Bühnenjahres (Velber, 1963), p. 66.

'*The Birthday Party* Filming to Start ', *The Times* (7 March, 1968), p. 7.

' The Filming of Pinter Plays ', *The Times* (9 January, 1968), p. 6.

' *The Homecoming* Awarded ', *The Times* (10 May, 1967), p. 1.

' *The Landscape* [cf. Palmer] To be Premiered on BBC ', *The Times,* (10 April, 1968), p. 13.

'1963 Television Awards', *The Times* (23 November, 1963), p.5.

'TV Programme on Pinter: Experiment in TV', *New York Times* (7 April, 1969), p.86.

Thomson, Philip, *The Grotesque* (London, 1972), pp. 29-32.

Thornton, Peter C., 'Blindness and the Confrontation with Death: Three Plays by Harold Pinter', *Die Neueren Sprachen,* 5 (1968), pp. 213-23.

Trewin, J.C., *Drama in Britain, 1951-1964* (London 1965).

Trilling, Ossia, 'The New English Realism', *Tulane Drama Review,* VII, 2 (Winter 1962), pp. 184-93.

Trilling, Ossia, 'Standort ungewiss. Uberblick der neuen englischen Dramatiker', *Theater der Zeit,* XV, 9 (1960), pp. 23-8.

Trilling, Ossia, 'The Young British Drama', *Modern Drama,* III, 2 (September 1960), pp. 168-77.

Trussler, Simon, *The Plays of Harold Pinter: an Assessment* (London 1973).

Tutaev, David, 'The Theatre of the Absurd . . . How Absurd?', *Gambit,* 2, 68-70.

Tynan, Kenneth, 'Dramatists in Perspective', *The Observer,* 15 September 1963, p. 27.

Tynan, Kenneth, 'Shouts and Murmurs', *The Observer,* 21 January 1968, p. 27.

Tynan, Kenneth, *Tynan on Theatre* (London, 1964).

Tynan, Kenneth, *Tynan Right and Left* (London, 1967).

Uhlmann, Wilfried, 'Neurotische Konflikte und triebgesteuertes Sozialverhalten in den Stucken Harold Pinters', *Literatur in Wissenschaft und Unterricht,* V, 4 (1972), pp. 299-312.

28

'University News', *The Times* (24 April, 1970), p.12.

'University News', *The Times* (18 January, 1971), p.14.

Vámos, László, and György Lengyel, 'László Vámos and György Lengyel Interviewed by Paul Neuburg', *Transatlantic Review*, 18 (Spring 1965), pp. 107-115.

Vannier, Jean, 'A Theatre of Language', *Tulane Drama Review,* VII, 3 (Spring 1963), pp. 180-6.

Vidan, Ivo, 'Komedija nespokpjstava', *Zagreb*, 9 (1963), pp. 462-73.

Volker, Klaus, 'Groteskformen des Theaters', *Akzente*, 4 (August 1960), pp. 321-39.

Wager, Walter, *The Playwright Speaks* (London, 1969).

Walker, Alexander, 'Magnificent, Yes - and Now I Know Why', *Evening Standard,* 16 July 1964.

Walker, Augusta, 'Messages from Pinter', *Modern Drama*, X, 1 (May 1967), pp. 1-10.

Walker, Augusta, 'Why the Lady Does It', in *A Casebook on Harold Pinter's The Homecoming*, ed. J. Lahr (New York, 1971), pp. 117-22.

Ward, A.C., *Twentieth Century English Literature* (London, 1964).

Wardle, Irving, 'A Director's Approach: an Interview with Peter Hall', in *A Casebook on Harold Pinter's The Homecoming*, ed. J. Lahr (New York, 1971), pp. 9-25.

Wardle, Irving, 'Comedy of Menace', *Encore*, V (September—October 1958), pp. 28-33. Reprinted in *The Encore Reader*, ed. C. Marowitz, T. Milne and O. Hale (London, 1965), pp. 86-91.

Wardle, Irving, 'Holding Up the Mirror', *Twentieth Century,* (Autumn 1964,) pp. 34-43.

Wardle, Irving, 'Revolt Against the West End', *Horizon*, V, 3 (January 1963), pp. 26-33.

Wardle, Irving, 'There's Music in That Room', *Encore*, VII, 3 (July—August 1960), pp. 32-4. Reprinted in *The Encore Reader*, ed. C. Marowitz, T. Milne and O. Hale (London, 1965), pp. 129-32.

Wardle, Irving, 'The Territorial Struggle', in *A Casebook on Harold Pinter's The Homecoming*, ed. J. Lahr (New York, 1971), pp. 37-44.

Warner, John, 'Can You Go Home Again: the Epistemological Quest in Pinter's *The Homecoming*', *Contemporary Literature*, 1970.

Wasson, Richard, 'Mime and Dream', *Pinter's Optics*, Midwest Monographs, I, 1 (September 1967), pp. 7-8.

Weightman, John, 'The Play as Fable', *Encounter*, (February 1967), p. 55.

Welland, Dennis, 'Some Post-War Experiments in Poetic Drama', in *Experimental Drama*, ed. W.A. Armstrong (London, 1963).

Wellwarth, George, *Contemporary Theatre* (New York, 1962).

Wellwarth, George, 'Harold Pinter: the Comedy of Allusiveness', in *The Theater of Protest and Paradox* (New York, 1964), pp. 197-211.

Wendt, Ernst,'Bürgerseelen und Randexistenzen: über die Dramatiker Harold Pinter und Franz Xaver Kroetz', in *Moderne Dramaturgie* (Frankfurt, 1974), pp. 91-117.

Whiting, John, 'Book Reviews', *London Magazine*, VII (November 1960), pp. 93-4. Reprinted in *The Art of the Dramatist* (London 1970), pp. 184-7.

Williams, Raymond, *'The Birthday Party:* Harold Pinter', in *Drama from Ibsen to Eliot* (London, 1968), pp. 322-5.

Williams, Raymond, 'Recent English Drama' in *The Pelican Guide to English Literature, Volume VII: The Modern Age,* ed. Boris Ford (Harmondsworth, 1964), pp. 496-508.

Wilson, Sheila, *Theatre of the Fifties* (London, 1963).

Winegarten, Renee, 'The Anglo-Jewish Dramatist in Search of His Soul', *Midstream,* XII, 8 (October 1966), pp. 40-52.

Worsley, T.C., 'A New Wave Rules Britannia', *Theatre Arts,* XLV, 10 (October 1961), pp. 17-19.

Worth, Katherine, J., 'Harold Pinter', in *Revolutions in Modern English Drama* (London, 1972), pp. 86-100.

Worth, Katherine J., 'Joyce via Pinter' in *Revolutions in Modern English Drama* (London, 1972), pp. 46-54.

Wortis, Irving, *'The Homecoming', Library Journal,* XCII (1 April 1967), p. 1508.

Wray, Phoebe, 'Pinter's Dialogue: the Play on Words', *Modern Drama,* XIII, 4 (February 1971), pp. 418-22.

Wright, Ian, 'Shooting *The Caretaker', Manchester Guardian,*(20 February 1963), p. 7.

Young, B.A. 'Pinter's Progress', *Financial Times,* 6 February 1971, p. 8.

Ziegler, Klaus, 'Das moderne Drama als Spiegel unserer Zeit', *Der Deutschunterricht,* 13 (1961), pp. 5-24.

Zolotow, Maurice, 'Young Man With Scorn', *New York Times,* 17 September, 1961, p. 1.

ADDENDA
To General Critical Material

Adler, Thomas P. 'Pinter's *Night:* A Stroll Down Memory Lane', *Modern Drama,* XVII, 4 (December, 1974), pp. 461-465.

Alexander, Nigel. 'Past, Present and Pinter', *Essays and Studies,* XXVII (1974), pp. 1-17.

Anderson, Michael; Jacques Guicharnaud, Kristin Morrison, Jack D. Zipes *et. al., A Handbook of Contemporary Drama* (London, repr. 1974), pp. 53-55; 281-283.

Aylwin, Tony. 'The Memory of All That: Pinter's *Old Times', English,* XXII (1973), pp. 99-102.

Barber, John. 'Harold Pinter, Conscious Alien', *Daily Telegraph* (3 May 1975), p. 14.

Barber, John. 'Pinter the Incomplete', *Daily Telegraph* (16 November, 1970), p. 6.

Brater, Enoch. 'Pinter's *Homecoming* on Celluloid', *Modern Drama,* XVII, 4 (December, 1974), pp. 443-448.

Brigg, Peter. 'The Understanding and Use of Time in the Plays of John Boynton Priestley, Samuel Beckett, and Harold Pinter', *Dissertation Abstracts International,* 32:6064A.

Brody, Alan. 'The Gift of Realism: Hitchock and Pinter', *Journal of Modern Literature,* III (1973), pp. 149-172.

Brooks, Mary Ellen. 'The British Theatre of Physical Despair', *Literature and Ideology,* 12 (1972), pp. 49-58.

Burghardt, Lorraine Hall. 'Game Playing in Three by Pinter', *Modern Drama,* XVII, 4 (December, 1974), pp. 377-388.

Carpenter, Charles. 'Harold Pinter', in: Hermann J. Weiand (ed.), *Insight IV* (Frankfurt/a.M., 1975), pp. 102-127.

Carpenter, Charles. ' 'What Have I Seen, the Scum or the Essence? ' Symbolic Fallout in Pinter's *Birthday Party', Modern Drama,* XXVII, 4 (December, 1974), pp. 389-402.

Clurman, Harold. *All People Are Famous: Instead of an Autobiography* (New York, 1974).

Clurman, Harold. *The Divine Pastime: Theatre Essays* (New York, 1974).

Craig, Alan. 'A Descriptive Analysis of Harold Pinter's Use of Comic Elements in His Stage Plays', *Dissertation Abstracts International,* 30:4597A.

Elsom, John. Erotic Theatre (New York, 1973).

English, Alan C. 'Feeling Pinter's World', *Ball State University Forum,* XIV, I (1973), pp. 70-75.

Flakes, Nanette S.B. 'Aesthetics of Modern Play Direction: Non-Realistic Drama from Pirandello to Pinter', *Dissertation Abstracts International,* 34:896A.

Garber, Stephen M. 'Open and Closed Sequences in the Plays of Harold Pinter', *Dissertation Abstracts International,* 34:312A-13Λ.

Gillen, Francis. ' 'All These Bits and Pieces'. Fragmentation and Choice in Pinter's Plays'. *Modern Drama,* XVII, 4 (December, 1974), pp. 477-487.

Goetsch, Paul. 'Harold Pinter: *Old Times*', in: H. Oppel (ed.), *Das englische Drama der Gegenwart* (Berlin, 1976).

Goodlad, J.S.R. *A Sociology of Popular Drama* (London, 1971).

Halbritter, Rudolf. *Konzeptionsformen des modernen angloamerikanischen Kurzdramas. Dargestellt an Stücken von W.B. Yeats, Th. Wilder und H. Pinter* (Göttingen, 1975).

Hall, Peter. Joseph, Losey and Harold Pinter, 'Crisis in the Film Industry', *The Times* (20 December 10, 1973), p. 17.

Hancock, Jim R. 'The Use of Time by Absurdist Playwrights: Beckett, Ionesco, Genet, and Pinter', *Dissertation Abstracts International*, 33:5876A.

'Harold Pinter, Director', *Cinebill*, I, 7 (January, 1974).

'Harold Pinter', *The Sunday Times* (13 May, 1973), p. 7.

Hayman, Ronald. 'Richard O'Callaghan', *The Times* (13 July, 1971), p. 7.

Hensel, Georg. *Theater der Zeitgenossen: Stücke und Autoren* (Frankfurt, Berlin, Wien, 1972), pp. 328-331.

Herin, Mariam M. 'An Analysis of Harold Pinter's Use of Language as Seen in *The Birthday Party, The Caretaker, The Homecoming*, and *Old Times, Dissertation Abstracts International*, 34:1913A.

Hinchliffe, Arnold P. *British Theatre 1950-70* (Oxford, 1974), pp. 127-141.

Holmes, Richard. 'Poetry International', *The Times* (June 22, 1972), p. 10.

Hughes, Alan. ' 'They Can't Take That away from Me': Myth and Memory in Pinter's *Old Times*', *Modern Drama*, XVII, 4 (December, 1974), pp. 467-476.

Imhof, Rüdiger. 'Forschungsberichte und Bibliographien zu Harold Pinter', *Anglia*, XCIII, 3/4 (1975), pp. 413-423.

Imhof, Rüdiger. 'Harold Pinters *revue sketches* als Schülletüre der gymnasialen Oberstufe (Sekundarstufe II)', *Die Neueren Sprache*, 5 (1975), pp. 390-401.

Imhof, Rüdiger. 'Harold Pinter: *The Dwarfs*', in: H. Priessnitz (ed.), *Das englische Hörspiel* (Düsseldorf, erscheint in 1977).

Imhof, Rüdiger. 'Pinter's *Silence:* The Impossibility of Communication', *Modern Drama*, XVII, 4 (December, 1974), pp. 449-460.

Jennings, Ann A. 'The Reaction of London's Drama Critics to Certain Plays by Henrik Ibsen, Harold Pinter, and Edward Bond', *Dissertation Abstracts International*, 34:2067A.

Jiji, Vera M. 'Pinter's Four Dimensional House: *The Homecoming:*, *Modern Drama*, XVII, 4 (December, 1974), pp. 433-442.

Jones, Edward T. 'Summer of 1900: A la recherche of *The Go-Between*', *Literature/Film Quarterly*, I (1973), pp. 154-160.

Jones, Paul D. 'The Intruder in the Drama of Harold Pinter: A Functional Analysis' *Dissertation Abstracts International*, 32:4759A.

Kähler, Klaus. *Die Syntax des Dialogs im modernen Englisch untersucht an Werken von Harold Pinter und Graham Green* (Diss. Berlin, Humboldt-Universität, 1973).

Kähler, Klaus. 'Die Syntax des Dialogs im modernen Englisch untersucht an Werken von Harold Pinter und Graham Green', *Zeitschrift für Anglistik und Amerikanistik*, XXIII, 1 (1975), pp. 41-63.

Kennedy, Andrew. *Six Dramatists in Search of a Language: Shaw, Eliot, Beckett, Pinter, Osborne, Arden* (Cambridge, 1975), pp. 165-191.

Lahr, John. 'Pinter and Chekhov: The Bond of Naturalism', in: ders., *Astonish Me* (New York, 1973), pp. 67-82.

Langley, Lee. 'Genius: A Change in Direction', *Daily Telegraph Magazine* (23 November, 1973), p. 30.

Lechler, Hans-Joachim. 'HaroldPinters Sketch: *Last To Go:* Untersuchungen zur Dialogführung', in: ders., *Lust und Unlust im Englischunterricht: Methodische Beispiele* (Stuttgart, 1972).

'Master of Silence: A Pinter Profile', *The Observer* (27 April, 1975), p. 11.

Miller, Mary Jane. 'Pinter as a Radio Dramatist', *Modern Drama*, XVII, 4 (December, 1974), pp. 403-412.

Morgan, Ricki. 'What Max and Teddy Come Home to in *The Homecoming*', *Educational Theatre Journal*, XXV (1973), pp. 490-499.

Muender, Peter. *Harold Pinter und die Problematik des absurden Theaters* (Bern, Frankfurt/a.M., 1975).

Murphy, Marese. 'Pinter and Visconti', *Drama*, 109 (Summer, 1973), p. 45.

Nichols, Peter. 'Mr. Pinter Accuses Signor Visconti of Staging 'Fiasco', *The Times* (11 May, 1973), pp. 1, 6.

Osherow, Anita R. 'Mother and Whore: The Role of Woman in *The Homecoming*', *Modern Drama*, XVII, 4 (December, 1974), pp. 423-432

'Peter Hall on Pinter', *Cinebill*, I, 2 (October, 1973).

'Producing Pinter: Peter Hall and John Bury . . . Talk to Michael McNay about Their Collaboration with the Playwright', *The Guardian* (1 June, 1971), p. 8.

Powlick, Leonard. 'A Phenomenological Approach to Harold Pinter's *A Slight Ache*', *Quarterly Journal of Speech*, LX (February, 1974), pp. 25-32.

Prentice, Penelope A. 'An Analysis of Dominance and Subservience as Technique and Theme in the Plays of Harold Pinter', *Dissertation Abstracts International*, 32:7000A.

Quigley, Austin E. *'The Dwarfs:* A Study in Linguistic Dwarfism', *Modern Drama,* XVII, 4 (December, 1974), pp. 413-422.

Quigley, Austin E. 'The Dynamics of Dialogue: The Plays of Harold Pinter', *Dissertation Abstracts International*, 33:6928A.

Quigley, Austin E. *The Pinter Problem* (Princeton, N.J., 1975).

Rusinko, Susan. 'Stratagems of Language in the Poems and Plays of Harold Pinter: A Study of Text, Sub-Text, and Conscious Sub-Text', *Dissertation Abstracts International*, 32:6451A.

Salem, Daniel. 'La blessure peuplée de Pinter', *Les Langues Modernes*, LXVII (1973), pp. 84-85.

Salem, Daniel. 'Le gardien: Analyse d'un personnage de Pinter', *Les Langues Modernes*, LXVII (1973), pp. 67-71.

Salem, James. *A Guide to Critical Reviews: Part III. British and Continental Drama from Ibsen to Pinter* (Metuchen, N.J., 1968).

Salom, Eric. 'Harold Pinter's Ear', *Modern Drama*, XVII, 4 (December 1974), pp. 363-375.

Schwarze, Hans-Wilhelm. 'Orientierungslosigkeit und Betroffensein. Spielelemente in Harold Pinters *The Birthday Party'*, *Literatur in Wissenschaft und Unterricht, VII*, 2 (August, 1974), pp. 98-114.

Steele, Richard. 'Britain: Hell Hath No Fury', *Newsweek* (11 August, 1975) pp. 18-19.

Stephens, Suzanne S. 'The Dual Influence: A Dramatic Study of the Plays of Edward Albee and the Specific Dramatic Forms and Themes which Influence Them', *Dissertation Abstracts International*, 34:342A.

Talley, Mary. 'The Relationship of Theme and Technique in the Plays of Harold Pinter', *Dissertation Abstracts International*, 33:1744A-1745A.

'Thames Scrap Play on Legal Advice', *The Times* (16 July, 1971), p. 12.

Toomey, Philippa. 'The Natural Theatre of Peter Hall', *The Times* (14 March, 1973), p. 19.

Towey, Denis F. 'Form and Content in Selected Plays of Harold Pinter', *Dissertation Abstracts International*, 34:3609A.

'Vienna Prize for Harold Pinter', *The Times* (16 November, 1973), p. 8.

Vos, Josef De. 'Harold Pinter: Praten tegen het niets', *Ons Erfdeel*, XVI, 4 (1973), pp. 118-119.

Weightman, John. 'Another Play for Pinterites', *Encounter* (July, 1975), pp. 24-26.

Wycisk, Max M. 'Language and Silence in the Stage Plays of Samuel Beckett and Harold Pinter', *Dissertation Abstracts International*, 33:4442A.

Zimmermann, Heinz. 'Harold Pinter: *The Birthday Party*', in: Klaus-Dieter Fehse und Norbert H. Platz (eds.), *Das zeitgenössiche englische Drama* (Frankfurt/a.M., 1975), pp. 43-70.

PRODUCTION REVIEWS

The Birthday Party on Stage

Alvarez, A. 'Death in the Morning', *New Statesman*, 12 December 1959, p. 836.

Barber, John, 'A Warning Perhaps, But a Bore', *Daily Express*, 20 May 1958, p. 12.

Barber, John. 'A Weird Comedy of Menace', *The Daily Telegraph* 9 January 1975. p. 14.

Barker, Felix. 'Prentice Pinter Revisited', *Evening News*, 9 January 1975. p. 16.

Billington, Michael. 'The Birthday Party', *The Guardian*, 9 January 1975, p. 10.

Bishop, George W., 'Zena Dare Says Farewell', *Daily Telegraph*, 28 April 1958, p. 11.

Boothroyd, J.B., 'At the Play', *Punch*, 28 May 1958, p. 720.

Brien, Alan, 'Communications', *The Spectator*, 30 May 1958, p. 687.

Brien, Alan, 'Pinter's First Play', *Sunday Telegraph*, 21 June 1964, p. 10.

Bryden, Ronald, 'Three Men in a Room', *New Statesman*, 26 June 1964, p. 1004. Reprinted in *The Unfinished Hero* (London, 1969), pp. 86-90.

C.L., '*The Birthday Party*', *Jewish Chronicle*, 23 May 1958, p. 26.

Cushman, Robert, 'True Love Conquers All - as Usual', *The Observer*, 19 January 1975, p. 29.

Darlington, W.A., 'Enjoyable Pinter', *Daily Telegraph*, 21 June 1964, p. 18.

Darlington, W.A., 'Mad Meg and Lodger', *Daily Telegraph*, 20 May 1958, p. 10.

Davenport, John, 'Pinter and Brecht', *Queen,* 1 July 1964, p. 8.

Dent, Alan, 'Mr. Pinter Misses His Target', *News Chronicle,* 20 May 1958, p. 5.

F.S., *'The Birthday Party'*, *Theatre World,* LX, 475 (August 1964), p. 13.

Gascoigne, Bamber, 'Pinter Makes It All Too Plain', *The Observer,* 21 June 1964, p. 24.

Granger, Derek, *'The Birthday Party'*,, *Financial Times,* 20 May 1958, p. 15.

G.R., 'Pinter's First Play Revived', *Time and Tide,* 28 July 1964, p. 28.

Gross, John, 'Amazing Reductions', *Encounter,* XXIII (September 1964), pp. 50-1.

Hall, Rodney, 'Theatre in London', *Westerly,* 3 (October 1964), pp. 57-60.

Hare, Norman, 'Miss Withers Saves the Show', *News Chronicle,* 22 March 1960, p. 5.

Hobson, Harold, 'A Change of Taste', *Sunday Times,* 24 July 1960, p. 31.

Hobson, Harold, 'Life Outside London', *Sunday Times,* 15 June 1958, p. 11.

Hobson, Harold, 'The Screw Turns Again', *Sunday Times,* 25 May 1958, p. 11.

Hope-Wallace, Philip, *'The Birthday Party* at the Aldwych', *The Guardian,* 19 June 1964, p. 11.

Itzin, Catherine. 'The Birthday Party', *Plays and Players,* XXII, 6 (March, 1975), pp. 26-27.

Jackson, Frank, 'The New Shows', *Sunday Citizen,* 25 May 1958, p. 7.

Jackson, Peter, *'The Birthday Party'*, *Plays and Players,* V, 10 (July 1958), p. 16.

Kingston, Jeremy, 'At the Play', *Punch,* 24 June 1964, p. 941.

Kretzmer, Herbert, 'The Laughs Grow - But Should Pinter Be Happy?', *Daily Express,* 19 June 1964, p. 6.

Lambert, J.W., 'Trial by Laughter', *Sunday Times,* 21 June 1964, p. 33.

'The Last Joke for the Phoenix Theatre', *The Times,* 12 September 1960, p. 3.

Levin, Bernard, 'The Last Laugh for Mr. Pinter?', *Daily Mail,* 19 June 1964, p. 14.

Lewis, Jack, 'Occult', *Sunday Citizen,* 21 June 1964, p. 20.

L.G.S., 'Comic Horror of *The Birthday Party'*, *The Stage,* 22 May 1958, p. 12.

L.M., *'The Birthday Party'*, *Theatre World,* LIV, 401 (June 1958), pp. 21, 23.

Marriott, R.B., 'Harold Pinter's First Play is Revived', *The Stage*, 25 June 1964, p. 13.

M.M.W., *'The Birthday Party', Manchester Guardian*, 21 May 1958, p. 5.

Myson, Mike, 'Horror 'Comic'', *Daily Worker*, 26 May 1958, p. 2.

Pacey, Ann, 'Pinter's Party Piece', *Daily Herald*, 19 June 1964, p. 5.

Pryce-Jones, Alan, 'The Party's Over', *Spectator*, 26 June 1964, p.854.

Purser, Philip, 'Mr. Bell's Farce Sums up a Revolution', *News Chronicle*, 25 April 1960, p. 3.

'Puzzling Surrealism of The *Birthday Party*', *The Times*, 20 May 1958, p. 3.

Shulman, Milton, 'Sorry, Mr. Pinter, You're Just Not Funny Enough', *Evening Standard*, 20 May 1958, p.6.

Shulman, Milton, 'The Party, Mr. Pinter, Is Beginning to Bore. . . ', *Evening Standard*, 19 June 1964, p. 4.

Shulman, Milton, 'Survival Course', *Evening Standard*, 9 January 1975, p. 21.

'A Slicker and Less Dangerous Pinter', *The Times*, 19 June 1964, p. 18.

Sutherland, Jack, 'Brilliant, Despairing Pinter', *Daily Worker*, 20 June, 1964, p. 3.

Taylor, J.R., 'Rags to Riches', *Plays and Players*, XI, 11 (August 1964), pp. 28 f.

Thirkell, Arthur, 'Birthday Shocker', *Daily Mirror*, 9 January, 1975, p. 16.

Thirkell, Arthur, 'First Night', *Daily Mirror*, 19 June, 1964, p. 18.

Trewin, J.C., 'After the Party', *Illustrated London News*, 31 May, 1958, p. 932.

Trewin, J.C., 'Guessing Game', *Illustrated London News*, 4 July 1964, p. 28.

Trewin, J.C., 'The New Plays', *Lady*, 5 June, 1958, p. 775.

"Two Young Playwrights Are Given a Chance", *The Times*, 19 May 1958, p. 14.

Tynan, Kenneth, 'Eastern Approaches', *The Observer*, 25 May 1958, p. 15.

Wardle, Irving, *'The Birthday Party', Encore*, V (July-August 1958), pp. 39-40.

Wardle, Irving, 'The Birthday Party', *The Times*, 9 January 1975, p. 12.

Wiggin, Maurice, 'Smaller But Sweeter', *The Sunday Times*, 27 March 1960, p. 23.

Wilson, Cecil, 'Cheers for the Mad Guest', *Daily Mail*, 20 May 1958, p. 3.

Worsley, T.C., 'A New Dramatist or Two', *New Statesman*, 31 May 1958, pp. 692, 694.

Wyndham, Francis, 'At the Theatre', *Queen*, 10 June 1958, p. 50.

Young, B.A., 'The Birthday Party', *The Financial Times*, 9 January 1975, p. 3.

The Birthday Party: Other References

Barnes, Clive, 'The Theatre: Pinter's *Birthday Party*', *New York Times*, 4 October 1967, p. 2.

Barlow, Graham, 'Plays and Players at Home: Manchester', *Plays and Players*, IX, 2 (November 1961), p. 34.

'Directors' Plays at Oxford', *The Times*, 28 November 1963, p. 17.

Hewes, Henry, 'Disobedience, Civil and Uncivil', *Saturday Review*, 28 October 1967, pp. 46-7.

Hews, Henry, 'Like Birth Warmed Over', *Saturday Review*, 21 October 1967, p. 50.

Parr, Ronald, 'Nottingham', *Plays and Players*, IX, 9 (June 1962), pp. 43 f.

'Two Pinter Plays for Broadway', *The Times*, August 1960, p. 5.

The Birthday Party on Television

Black, Peter, 'Peter Black's Teleview', *Daily Mail*, 23 March 1960, p. 16.

Cooke, Fred, 'Mystery', *Reynolds News*, 27 March 1960, p. 11.

Coton, A.V., 'What Was the Matter With Stanley', *Daily Telegraph*, 23 March 1960, p. 14.

Diack, Phil, 'A Stage Flop is Big Hit', *Daily Herald*, 23 March 1960, p. 5.

Lane, Stewart, 'An Eerie Affair', *Daily Worker*, 24 March 1960, p. 2.

Richardson, Maurice, 'Oedipus of the Sixth Form', *The Observer*, 27 March 1960, p. 25.

Sear, Richard, 'A Play to Scorch Nerve Ends', *Daily Mirror*, 23 March 1960, p. 18.

'A Simple Play: *The Birthday Party* on Television', *The Times*, 23 March 1960, p. 16.

The Birthday Party as a Film

Coleman, John, 'Pinter's Party Pictured', *New Statesman*, 20 February 1970, p. 267.

'Filming *The Birthday Party*', *The Times*, 7 March 1968, p. 7.

Gow, Gordon, '*The Birthday Party*', *Films and Filming*, XVI, 7 (April 1970), p. 41.

Mallett, Richard, 'At the Cinema', *Punch,* 18 February 1970, p. 276.

P.H.S., 'Americans Film Pinter', *The Times,* 9 January 1968, p. 6.

Pritchett, Oliver, 'Fried-Up Pinter', *The Guardian,* 27 April 1968, p. 7.

The Room and The Dumb Waiter on Stage

Alvarez, A., 'Wanted—a Language', *New Statesman,* 30 January 1960, pp. 149-50.

Barnes, Clive, 'A Mystery That Asks All the Questions', *Daily Express,* 9 March 1960, p. 17.

Brien, Alan, 'The Guilty Seam', *The Spectator,* 29 January 1960, p. 137.

Cain, Alex Matheson, 'Critics' Column', *Tablet,* 19 March 1960, p. 272.

C.L., 'Double Bill', *Jewish Chronicle,* 18 March 1960, p. 39.

Darlington, W.A., 'Cross-Talk Good, Point Unknown', *Daily Telegraph,* 22 January 1960, p. 14.

Findlater, Richard, 'Theatre', *Time and Tide,* 19 March 1960, p. 314.

Findlater, Richard, *'The Room, The Dumb Waiter', Financial Times,* 22 January 1960, p. 17.

'First Play by Mr. Pinter: *The Room* Excusably Derivative', *The Times,* 9 March 1960, p. 4.

F.S., *'The Dumb Waiter* and *The Room', Theatre World,* LVI, 423 (April 1960), p. 8.

Gibbs, Patrick, 'People Shut in a Private World', *Daily Telegraph,* 9 March 1960, p. 14.

Gilliatt, Penelope, 'Interview With a Marathon Critic Nearing Wit's End', *Queen,* 30 March 1960, p. 18.

Hobson, Harold, *'The Dumb Waiter, The Room', The Sunday Times,* 13 March 1960, p. 25.

Hobson, Harold, 'Theatre', *The Sunday Times,* 24 January 1960, p. 23.

Hobson, Harold, 'Vagaries of the West End', *The Sunday Times,* 31 January 1960, p. 23.

Hope-Wallace, Philip, *'The Dumb Waiter, The Room', Manchester Guardian,* 10 March 1960, p. 9.

Keown, Eric, 'At the Play', *Punch,* 16 March 1960, p. 400.

Lambert, J.W., 'Plays in Performance', *Drama,* 56 (Spring 1960), pp. 20-7.

Levin, Bernard, 'Nowhither and Doing Nowhat', *Daily Express,* 22 January 1960, p. 4.

Milne, Tom, 'Double Pinter', *Encore,* VII, 2 (1960), pp. 38-40.

Mortlock, C.B., 'She's a Poppet', *City Press,* 18 March 1960, p. 8.

Pryce-Jones, Alan, 'At the Theatre', *The Observer*, 24 January 1960, p. 21.

Pryce-Jones, Alan, 'Mathematics of the Heart', *The Observer*, 13 March 1960, p. 23.

Richardson, Maurice, 'The Pilkington Network', *The Observer*, 8 October 1961, p. 27.

Roberts, Peter, *'The Dumb Waiter, The Room'*, *Plays and Players*, VII, 7 (April 1960), p. 16.

'Strange and Subtle Double Bill', *The Times*, 22 January 1960, p. 6.

Trewin, J.C., 'The New Plays', *Lady*, 4 February 1960, pp. 150 f.

Trewin, J.C., 'The Right Approach', *Illustrated London News*, 19 March 1960, p. 486.

Trewin, J.C., 'Thick and Clear', *Illustrated London News*, 6 February 1960, p. 226.

Walker, Alexander, 'These Two Will Set You Puzzling', *Evening Standard*, 9 March 1960, p. 10.

Wilson, Cecil, 'Pinter Better in Halves', *Daily Mirror*, 9 March 1960, p. 3.

Worsley, T.C., *'The Room, The Dumb Waiter'*, The Financial Times, 9 March 1960, p. 17.

W.W., 'Two Bafflers', *Daily Worker*, 10 March 1960, p. 2.

A Night Out on Radio

'Comically Dreadful World', *The Times*, 2 March 1960, p. 13.

Ferris, Paul, 'Fresh and Bloody', *The Observer*, 6 March 1960, p. 23.

'Mr. Pinter's Night Out', *The Times*, 2 March 1960, p. 13.

A Night Out on Television

Black, Peter, 'Mr. Pinter Again — But Not So Obscure', *Daily Mail*, 25 April 1960, p. 16.

King, Francis, 'Television', *The Listener*, 1978 (23 February 1967), p. 271.

Lane, Stewart, 'Talented Harold Pinter', *Daily Worker*, 26 April 1960, p. 3.

Lockhardt, Freda Bruce, 'Television', *Time and Tide*, 30 April 1960, p. 483.

'Pinter Play on Television', *The Times*, 25 April 1960, p. 16.

Richardson, Maurice, 'Rope's End and Stop Watch', *The Observer*, 4 May 1960, p. 19.

Sear, Richard, *'A Night Out'*, *Daily Mirror*, 25 April 1960, p. 26.

Turton, Henry, 'On the Air', *Punch*, 4 May 1960, p. 629.

A Night Out on Stage

Brien, Alan, 'A Pinter Week', *Sunday Telegraph*, 8 October 1961, p. 10.

Darlington, W.A., 'Jekyll-Hyde Pinter', *Daily Telegraph*, 3 October 1961, p. 14.

Findlater, Richard, 'Doubling the Pleasure', *Time and Tide*, 12 October 1961, p. 1701.

Gellert, Roger, 'Religion and Sex', *New Statesman*, 13 October 1961, pp. 529 f.

Hope-Wallace, Philip, 'Three From Dublin', *The Guardian*, 3 October 1961, p. 7.

J.S., 'Counter-Point', *Daily Worker*, 4 October 1961, p.2.

Lewis, Jack, 'Shaw Has Plenty of Ideas for 1961', *Reynolds News*, 8 October 1961, p. 11.

Lewis, Peter, 'A Small Pinter But Deftly Done', *Daily Mail*, 3 October 1961, p. 3.

Piler, Jack, 'Pinter's Play Makes a Real 'Night Out' ', *Daily Herald*, 3 October 1961, p. 9.

'Psychological Truth in Pinter's Play', *The Times*, 3 October 1961, p. 16.

Shulman, Milton, 'Terrifying – This Hymn of Hate Against Women', *Evening Standard*, 3 October 1961, p. 18.

The Caretaker on Stage

Alvarez, A., 'Olivier Among the Rhinos', *New Statesman*, 7 May 1960, pp. 666-7.

Arden, John, *'The Caretaker'*, *New Theatre Magazine*, 4 (July 1960), pp. 29-30.

Barber, John, 'Brilliant Revival of *The Caretaker'*, *Daily Telegraph*, 3 March 1972, p. 11.

Bentley, Jack, 'The Week's New Shows', *Sunday Pictorial*, 1 May 1960, p. 21.

Billington, Michael, *'The Caretaker'*, *The Guardian*, 3 March 1972, p. 8.

Bishop, George W., 'Mr. Pinter Won't Answer', *Daily Telegraph*, 25 April 1960, p. 15.

Brien, Alan, 'Chelsea Beaujolais', *The Spectator*, 6 May 1960, p. 661.

Brien, Alan, 'Something Blue', *The Spectator*, 10 June 1960, pp. 835-6.

Carthew, Anthony, 'This is the Best Play in London', *Daily Herald*, 28 April 1960, p. 3.

Coleman, John, 'The Road to Sidcup', *New Statesman*, 13 March 1964, p. 423.

Coward, Noel, 'These Old-Fashioned Revolutionaries', *Daily Herald*, 28 April 1960, p. 3.

Darlington, W.A., 'Actability of Harold Pinter', *Daily Telegraph*, 31 May 1960, p. 14.

Dennis, Nigel, 'Optical Delusions', *Encounter*, XV (July 1960), pp.63-6.

Dent, Alan, 'Tragedy of a Tramp Alarms Me', *News Chronicle*, 31 May 1960, p. 3.

Donoghue, Denis, 'London Letter: Moral West End', *Hudson Review*, (Spring 1961), pp. 93-103.

F.G., 'Innocuous Revue', *Jewish Chronicle*, 6 May 1960, p. 34.

Findlater, Richard, 'Theatre', *Time and Tide*, 7 May 1960, p. 509.

Frame, Colin, *'The Caretaker'*, *Evening News*, 3 March 1972, p. 3.

Gibbs, Patrick, 'Mr. Pinter Returns to Enigma', *Daily Telegraph*, 28 April 1960, p. 14.

Gilderdale, Michael, 'Spellbinder Made of Three Men', *News Chronicle*, 28 April 1960, p. 3.

Gilliatt, Penelope, 'Comedy of Menace', *Queen*, 25 May 1960, pp. 21-2.

H.G.M., *'The Caretaker'*, *Theatre World*, LVI, 425 (June 1960), pp. 8-9.

Hobson, Harold, 'A Change of Taste', *The Sunday Times*, 24 July 1960, p. 31.

Hobson, Harold, 'Real and Romantic Agony', *The Sunday Times*, 5 March 1972, p. 34.

Hobson, Harold, 'Things Are Looking Up', *The Sunday Times*, 5 June 1960, p. 25.

Keown, Eric, 'At the Play', *Punch*, 11 May 1960, p. 665.

Kretzmer, Herbert, 'Fight Against Time by New *Caretaker'*, *Daily Express*, 3 March 1972, p. 12.

Lambert, J.W., 'Plays in Performance', *Drama*, 57 (Summer 1960), pp. 18-25.

Lambert, J.W., *'The Caretaker'*, *The Sunday Times*, 1 May 1960, p. 25.

Levin, Bernard, 'Three-Line Cut Lets Everyone See This Play', *Daily Express*, 31 May 1960, p. 16.

Levin, Bernard, 'There's Truth in This Man's Every Twitch', *Daily Express*, 2 May 1960, p. 4.

Lewis, Peter, *'The Caretaker'*, *Daily Mail*, 3 March 1972, p. 19.

Mannes, Marya, 'Just Looking, Thanks', *Reporter*, 13 October 1960, pp. 48-51.

Marowitz, Charles, *'The Caretaker'*, in *Confessions of a Counterfeit Critic* (London, 1973), pp. 47-9.

M.M., 'A Collection of Characters', *Daily Worker*, 26 April 1960, p. 2.

Mortimer, John, 'Now This Is What I Call Great Acting', *Evening Standard*, 31 May 1960, p. 12.

Mortlock, C.B., 'Sir Laurence With No Heroics', *City Press*, 16 May 1960, p. 13.

Mortlock, C.B., 'Two Casualties', *City Press*, 3 June 1960, p. 10.

'Mr. Pinter Takes Over in *The Caretaker*', *The Times*, 21 February 1961, p. 15.

Muller, Robert, 'The Small World of Harold Pinter', *Daily Mail*, 30 April, 1960, p. 3.

Panter-Downes, Mollie, 'Letter from London', *New Yorker*, XXXVI (9 July 1960), pp. 57-61.

Pryce-Jones, Alan, 'Through the Looking Glass', *The Observer*, 5 May 1960, p. 23.

Richards, Dick, 'Subtle Goonery', *Daily Mirror*, 31 May 1960, p. 18.

Roberts, Peter, *'The Caretaker'*, *Plays and Players*, VII, 10 (July 1960), p. 15.

R.B.M., 'Mr. Pinter Has Written a Fine Play in *The Caretaker*', *The Stage*, 5 May 1960, p. 21.

'Mr. Pinter Takes over in *The Caretaker*', *The Times*, 21 February 1961, p. 15.

Rosselli, John, 'Between Farce and Madness', *Manchester Guardian*, 29 April 1960, p. 13.

'A Slight Play that Pleases and Dazes', *The Times*, 28 April 1960, p. 6.

Smith, Lisa G., *'The Caretaker'*, *Plays and Players*, VII, 9 (June 1960), p. 17.

'The Caretaker's New Home', *The Times*, 31 May 1960, p. 4.

Thirkell, Arthur, 'Gales of Mirth', *Daily Mirror*, 3 March 1972, p. 16.

Trewin, J.C., 'Battle Area', *Illustrated London News*, 11 June 1960, p. 1036.

Trewin, J.C., 'Four in Hand', *Illustrated London News*, 14 May 1960, p. 850.

Trewin, J.C., 'The New Plays', *Lady*, 12 May 1960, pp. 715-6.

Tynan, Kenneth, 'A Verbal Wizard in the Suburbs', *The Observer*, 5 June 1960, p. 17.

Wardle, Irving, *'The Caretaker'*, *The Times*, 3 March 1972, p. 11.

West, Richard, 'Extraordinary', *Daily Mirror*, 28 April 1960, p. 26.

Worsley, T.C., *'The Caretaker'*, *Financial Times*, 28 April 1960, p. 19.

The Caretaker: Other References

'American Taste in British Plays of Today', *The Times*, 15 November 1961, p. 19.

Brunius, Joseph, 'Pinter in Paris', *Plays and Players*, VIII, 9 (June 1961), p. 3.

Calas, Andre, 'Plays and Players Abroad: Paris', *Plays and Players*, VIII, 6 (March 1961), p. 31.

'Cheaper New York Prices for *The Caretaker*', *The Times*, 26 August 1961, p. 10.

Colin, Saul, 'Plays and Players in New York', *Plays and Players*, IX, 3 (December 1961), p. 19.

'Destruction of a Tramp', *The Times*, 11 February 1964, p. 13.

Dibb, Frank, 'Plays and Players at Home: Birmingham', *Plays and Players*, IX, 2 (November 1961), p. 35.

Dibb, Frank, 'Plays and Players at Home: Oxford', *Plays and Players*, IX, 4 (January 1962), p. 27.

Hewes, Henry, 'Nothing Up the Sleeve', *Saturday Review*, 21 October 1961, p. 20.

'High Praise for Mr. Pinter: New York Likes *The Caretaker*', *The Times*, 6 October 1961, p. 34.

Kahl, Kurt, 'Harold Pinter: *Der Hausmeister*', *Theater Heute*, III, 5 (1962), p. 48.

Koegler, Horst, 'Plays and Players Abroad: Dusseldorf', *Plays and Players*, VIII, 8 (May 1961), p. 17.

Lubbren, Rainer, 'Das ABC des Hausmeisters', *Theater und Zeit*, 9 (1961-62), pp. 245-51.

Schumacher, Ernst, 'In Munchen *Der Hausmeister* von Harold Pinter', *Theater der Zeit*, XVI, 4 (1961), pp. 70-1.

Taubman, Harold, 'A Leap Forward: Pinter Makes Progress in Caretakers', *New York Times*, 15 October 1961, p. 1.

'Two Pinter Plays for Broadway', *The Times*, 12 August 1960, p. 5.

The Caretaker on Radio

Rodger, Ian, 'The Wrong Audience', *The Listener*, 29 March 1962, p. 573.

The Caretaker as a Film

Butcher, Maryvonne, 'Achtung', *Tablet*, 14 March, p. 301-2.

Cutts, John, *'The Caretaker'*, *Films and Filming*, X, 4 (January 1964), pp. 24-5.

Dent, Alan, 'Two Grisly Experiences', *Illustrated London News*, 28 March 1964, p. 502.

Donner, Clive, 'The Caretaker', Sight and Sound, XXXIII, 2 (Spring 1964), pp. 64-5.

Gibbs, Patrick, 'The Caretaker in Close-Up', Daily Telegraph, 13 March 1964, p. 13.

Gilliatt, Penelope, 'The Conversion of a Tramp', The Observer, 15 March 1964, p. 24.

Hibbin, Nina, 'Wistful, Engaging - But in the End a Bore', Daily Worker, 14 March 1964, p. 3.

J.F., 'Pinter Masterpiece', Jewish Chronicle, 13 March 1964, p. 48.

Lewis, Jack, 'Theatre and Cinema', Sunday Citizen, 15 March 1964, p. 24.

Mallett, Richard, 'At the Pictures', Punch, 25 March 1964, p. 468.

Mosley, Leonard, 'Three So Splendid', Daily Express, 12 March 1964, p. 4.

Oakes, Philip, 'Pinter's Worthy Poineer', The Sunday Telegraph, 15 March 1964, p. 14.

Pacey, Ann, 'Three Men in a House of Dreams', Daily Herald, 13 March 1964, p. 6.

Powell, Dilys, 'Solitaries in an Attic', The Sunday Times, 15 March 1964, p. 33.

'Pinter Writes His Own Film Script', The Times, 10 March 1964, p. 15.

Quigley, Isabel, 'Pinter's Marks', The Spectator, 20 March 1964, p. 381.

Richardson, Gina, 'Taking Care', Time and Tide, 19-25 March 1964, p. 37.

Robinson, David, 'Trios', Financial Times, 13 March 1964, p. 26.

Sale, James, 'The Film of the Play', Queen, 11 March 1964, p. 17.

Taylor, J.R., 'The Servant and The Caretaker', Sight and Sound, XXXIII, 1 (Winter 1963-64), pp. 38-9.

Walker, Alexander, 'Brilliant . . . and Disappointing', Evening Standard, 12 March 1964, p. 10.

Wilson, Cecil, 'Why I'm Saying Thank You, Liz, This Morning', Daily Mail, 10 March 1964, p. 18.

Wiseman, Thomas, 'Harold Pinter's The Caretaker', Sunday Express, 15 March 1964, p. 23.

Night School on Television

Forster, Peter, 'Inconsequences', The Spectator, 29 July 1960, p. 186.

Lewis, Peter, 'Straightforward? Well, No, But Highly Entertaining', Daily Mail, 22 July 1960, p. 14.

'Mr. Pinter's Concession', The Times, 22 July 1960, p. 16.

Phillips, Philip, 'It's a Pity I Couldn't Laugh Last Night', Daily Herald,

22 July 1960, p. 3.

Richardson, Maurice, 'Mr. Pinter's Night Thoughts', *The Observer,* 24 July 1960, p. 24.

Sear, Richard, 'Diamond Bright Comedy', *Daily Mirror,* 22 July 1960, p. 16.

Turton, Henry, 'On the Air', *Punch,* 3 August 1960, p. 174.

Wiggin, Maurice, 'I Have Been Here Before', *The Sunday Times,* 24 July, 1960, p. 36.

Young, Kenneth, 'Comedy of a Night Club 'Chick': Wry Mr. Pinter', *Daily Telegraph,* 22 July 1960. p. 15.

A Slight Ache on Radio

Cain, Alex Matheson, 'Words of Fantasy', *Tablet,* 25 February 1961, p. 178.

'Commonplace into Fantasy', *The Times,* 30 July 1959, p. 8.

Ferris, Paul, 'Radio Notes', *The Observer,* 2 August 1959, p. 12.

Robinson, Robert, 'With Proper Humility', *The Sunday Times,* 2 August 1959, p. 14.

A Slight Ache on Stage

Carthew, Peter, 'Three', *Plays and Players,* VIII, 6 (March 1961), p. 11.

Craig, H.A.L., 'The Sound of the Words', *New Statesman,* 27 January 1961, pp. 152-3.

Darlington, W.A., 'Pinter Plays Obscurity', *Daily Telegraph,* 19 January 1961, p. 14.

'Entertaining Triple Bill', *The Times,* 19 January 1961, p. 16.

Findlater, Richard, 'In the Deep Freeze', *Time and Tide,* 27 January 1961, p. 130.

F.S., 'Three', *Theatre World,* LVII, 433 (February 1961), p. 16.

Gascoigne, Bamber, 'Pulling the Wool?', *The Spectator,* 27 January 1961, p. 106.

Gilbert, W. Stephen, 'A Slight Ache, Landscape', *Plays and Players,* XXI, 3 (December 1973), pp. 52-3.

Gilliatt, Penelope, 'Beefing About Opera', *Queen,* 1 February 1961, p. 15.

Hobson, Harold, 'The Arts in Form Again', *The Sunday Times,* 22 January 1961, p. 33.

Hope-Wallace, Philip, 'Treble Chance', *The Guardian,* 19 January 1961, p. 9.

Keown, Eric, 'At the Play', *Punch,* 25 January 1961, p. 186.

Lambert, J.W., 'Plays in Performance', *Drama,* 60 (Spring 1961), pp. 20-6.

Levin, Bernard, 'One Times Three is a Sum That Pleases Me', *Daily Express*, 19 January 1961 p. 8.

Marriott, R.B., 'Mortimer, Simpson, and Pinter, All in One Evening', *The Stage*, 26 January 1961, p. 13.

M.M., 'Three', *Daily Worker*, 20 January 1961, p. 2.

Muller, Robert, 'Hate Yourself Though You May, You'll Enjoy These Plays', *Daily Mail*, 19 January 1961, p. 3.

Nathan, David, 'This is Life Over the Hill', *Daily Herald*, 19 January 1961, p. 3.

Shulman, Milton, 'The Terror', *Evening Standard*, 19 January 1961, p. 14.

'The Reaction Against Realism', *Times Literary Supplement* 30 June 1961, p. 400.

Trewin, J.C., 'Cutting It Short', *Illustrated London News*, 4 February 1961, p. 192.

Tynan, Kenneth, 'Let Coward Flinch', *The Observer*, 22 January 1961, p. 30.

Worsley, T.C., 'Three Plays at the Arts', *The Financial Times*, 19 January 1961, p. 17.

The Collection on Television

'Ambiguity', *Times Literary Supplement*, 12 May 1961, p. 296.

Black, Peter, 'Peter Black's Teleview', *Daily Mail*, 12 May 1961, p. 3.

Diack, Phil, 'Put it in the Drawer, Pinter!', *Daily Herald*, 12 May 1961, p. 4.

'Lightweight But Lively Pinter', *The Times*, 12 May 1961, p. 19.

Purser, Philip, 'Pinter's Boxes', *Sunday Telegraph*, 14 May 1961, p. 10.

Richardson, Maurice, 'Eyes Behind the Iron Curtain', *The Observer*, 14 May 1961, p. 27.

Sear, Richard, 'A Glittering Haze', *Daily Mirror*, 12 May 1961, p. 20.

Shorter, Eric, 'Pinter Up in the World', *Daily Telegraph*, 12 May 1961, p. 17.

Wiggin, Maurice, 'Rag Trade', *The Sunday Times*, 14 May 1961, p. 48.

The Collection on Radio

Lewis, Naomi, 'Experiments in Listening', *The Observer*, 17 June 1962, p. 24.

Shuttleworth, Martin, 'Ambiguities', *The Listener*, 21 June 1962, pp. 1089-90.

Wilsher, Peter, 'What Happened in Leeds?', *The Sunday Times*, 17 June 1962, p. 44.

The Collection on Stage

Barker, Felix, 'Pinter's Pregnant Pauses', *Evening News,* 19 June 1962, p. 5.

Brien, Alan, 'Better in the Box', *Sunday Telegraph,* 24 June 1962, p.8.

Cain, Alex Matheson, 'Strange Menaces', *Tablet,* 30 June 1962, p. 624.

C.L., 'Pinter's Humour', *Jewish Chronicle,* 22 June 1962, p. 30.

Darlington, W.A., 'Mr. Pinter's Might-Have-Been', *Daily Telegraph,* 19 June 1962, p. 14.

'Empty', *Daily Mirror,* 19 June 1962, p. 24.

Foreman, Carl, 'Majors and Minors', *New Statesman,* 22 June 1962, p. 917.

Gascoigne, Bamber, 'Cult of Personality', *The Spectator,* 29 June 1962, p. 854.

H.G.M., *'The Collection* and *Playing With Fire',* *Theatre World,* LVIII, 45 (August 1962), p. 6.

Higgins, John, *'The Collection',* *The Financial Times,* 19 June 1962, p. 20.

Hope-Wallace, Philip, 'New Pinter Play', *The Guardian,* 19 June 1962, p. 7.

Keown, Eric, 'At the Play', *Punch,* 22 June 1962, p. 987.

Kretzmer, Herbert, 'The Magic Touch That Falters', *Daily Express,* 19 June 1962, p. 4.

Lambert, J.W., 'A Stitch in Time', *The Sunday Times,* 24 June 1962, p. 35.

Lambert, J.W., 'Plays in Performance', *Drama,* 66 (Autumn 1962), pp. 18-25.

Lewis, Jack, 'The Value of Virtue', *Reynolds News,* 24 June 1962, p. 8.

Marriott, R.B., 'Strindberg's Couples, Pinter's Too', *The Stage,* 21 June 1962, p. 13.

Mayersberg, Paul, 'Harold Pinter's *The Collection',* *The Listener,* 5 July 1962, p. 26.

Muller, Robert, 'An Evening Like This Revives One's Faith', *Daily Mail.* 19 June 1962, p. 3.

Nathan, David, 'Pinter Looks at Loving', *Daily Herald,* 19 June 1962, p. 7.

'On the Fence Between Farce and Tragedy', *The Times,* 19 June 1962, p. 13.

Ryan, Stephen P., 'The London Stage', *America,* CVII (27 October 1962), pp. 956-8.

Shulman, Milton, 'Pinter in His Best Hypnotic Mood', *Evening Standard* 19 June 1962, p. 10.

Sigal, Clancy, 'The Collection', Queen, 3 July 1962, p. 17.

Taylor, J.R., 'Cuckoo in the Nest', Plays and Players, IX, 11 (August 1962), pp. 20 f.

Thirkell, Arthur, 'Empty', Daily Mirror, 19 June 1962, p. 24.

Thompson, H., 'A Slight Case of Conversation', The Times, 23 June 1962, p. 4.

Trewin, J.C., 'Between the Lines', Illustrated London News, 30 June 1962, p. 1058.

Trewin, J.C., 'New Plays', Lady, 5 July 1962, pp. 2-3.

Wardle, Irving, 'Laughter in the Wilderness', The Observer, 24 June 1962, p. 23.

Wiseman, Thomas, 'A Life on the Old Ocean Wave', Time and Tide, 28 June 1962, pp. 13-14.

The Lover on Television

'Autumn Plays for New Arts Theatre', The Times, 10 April 1963, p. 15.

'Award for Pinter Play', The Times (October, 1963), p. 15.

Bill, Jack, 'A Too-Sexy Pinter?', Daily Mirror, 28 March 1963, p. 18.

Bourne, Richard, 'New Pinter on Television', The Guardian, 29 March 1963, p. 9.

'Complex Design of Marriage', The Times, 29 March 1963, p. 15.

Gowers, Michael, 'Freud, No Doubt, Had the Word', Daily Mail, 29 March 1963, p. 18.

Lane, Stewart, 'New Director? Let's Call in the Head Shrinker', Daily Worker, 30 March 1963, p. 2.

Leonard, Hugh, 'Television Plays ', Plays and Players, X, 9 (June 1963), p. 41.

Lockwood, Lyn, 'Pinter's Play's Message is Received', Daily Telegraph, 29 March 1963, p. 16.

'Pinter's Lovers', The Stage, 28 March 1963, p. 1.

'Pinter Play Features Some Variations on Marital Theme', The Stage, 4 April 1963, p. 11.

Potter, Dennis, 'Pinter Play a Sizzling Triumph', Daily Herald, 29 March 1963, p. 7.

Purser, Philip, 'Middle View', The Sunday Telegraph, 31 March 1963, p. 13.

Richardson, Maurice, 'Pinter Among the Pigeons', The Observer, 31 March 1963, p. 39.

Sear, Richard, 'Such an Elegant Love Play', Daily Mirror, 29 March 1963, p. 18.

Walsh, Michael, 'One Fine Hour With Pinter's Lovers', *Daily Express,* 29 March 1963, p. 4.

Wiggin, Maurice, 'Crime and Punishment', *The Sunday Times,* 31 March 1963, p. 39.

The Dwarfs on Radio

Ferris, Paul, 'Radio Notes', *The Observer,* 11 December 1960, p. 26.

Laws, Frederick, 'Man of Blood', *The Listener,* 8 December 1960, p. 1078.

Robinson, Robert, 'Radio', *The Sunday Times,* 25 December 1960, p. 32.

'Mr. Pinter at His Most Subtle', *The Times* 3 December 1960, p. 10.

The Lover and The Dwarfs on Stage

Bernhard, F.J., 'English Theatre 1963: In the Wake of the New Wave', *Books Abroad,* Spring 1964, pp. 143-4.

Boothroyd, Basil, 'At the Play', *Punch,* 25 September 1963, p. 467.

Brahms, Caryl, 'The Silence of the Pope', *Time and Tide,* 3-9 October 1963, p. 33.

Browne, E. Martin,'A Peep at the English Theatre, Fall 1963', *Drama Survey,* III (February 1964), pp. 413-6.

Bryden, Ronald, 'Atavism', *New Statesman,* 27 September 1963, p. 420.

Darlington, W.A., 'Pinter at His Most Pinteresque', *Daily Telegraph,* 19 September 1963, p. 16.

Forster, Peter, 'Back to the Saltmines', *The Sunday Telegraph,* 22 September 1963, p. 12.

F.S., *'The Lover* and *The Dwarfs',* *Theatre World,* LIX, 465 (October 1963), pp. 10-11.

Gascoigne, Bamber, 'Love in the Afternoon', *The Observer,* 22 September 1963, p. 26.

Hall, Stuart, *'The Lover* and *The Dwarfs',* *Encore,* X, 6 (November—December 1963), pp. 47-9.

Hobson, Harold, 'The Importance of Fantasy', *The Sunday Times,* 22 September 1963, p. 33.

Hope-Wallace, Philip, 'Two Pinter Plays at the New Arts', *The Guardian* 19 September 1963, p. 9.

J.F., 'Unforgettable Stage Experience', *Jewish Chronicle,* 27 September 1963, p. 42.

J.F., 'Pinter and the Malignant Dwarfs', *Daily Worker,* 20 September 1963, p. 2.

Kee, Robert, *'The Lover* and *The Dwarfs'*, *Queen*, 9 October 1963, p. 16.

Kretzmer, Herbert, 'Freaky Night at the Pinter Mime', *Daily Express*, 19 September 1963, p. 4.

Lambert, J.W., 'Plays in Performance', *Drama*, 71 (Winter 1963), pp. 18-26.

Levin, Bernard, 'And My Index Finger Itches', *Daily Mail*, 19 September 1963, p. 3.

Lewis, Jack, 'The Little Man's Secret Urge to Kill', *Sunday Citizen*, 22 September 1963, p. 22.

Marriott, R.B., 'Pinter Double Bill: *The Lover* and *The Dwarfs'*, *The Stage*, 26 September 1963, p. 13.

'Mr. Pinter's Double Bill', *The Times*, 20 June 1963, p. 16.

'Mr. Pinter Pursues an Elusive Reality', *The Times*, 19 September p. 16.

Nathan, David, 'Pinter's Poetic But Puzzling Private World', *Daily Herald*, 19 September 1963, p. 3.

'Pinter's Demon Lover Is a Husband', *Evening News*, 19 September 1963, p. 4.

Pryce-Jones, D., 'Myths in the Living Room', *Spectator*, 27 September 1963, p. 386.

Shulman, Milton, 'The Private, Padded World of Mr. Pinter', *Evening Standard*, 19 September 1963, p. 4.

Taylor, J.R., 'Half Pints of Pinter', *Plays and Players*, XI, 2 (November 1963), pp. 38-9.

Thirkell, Arthur, 'First Night', *Daily Mirror*, 19 September 1963, p. 18.

Thompson, H., 'Mr. Pinter Pursues an Elusive Reality', *The Times*, 19 September 1963, p. 16.

Trewin, J.C., 'Mixed Drinks', *Illustrated London News*, 5 October 1963, p. 526.

Trewin, J.C., 'The New Plays', *Lady*, 3 October 1963, p. 441.

Worsley, T.C., *'The Lover* and *The Dwarfs'*, *The Financial Times*, 19 September 1963, p. 22.

The Homecoming on Stage

Barker, Felix, 'The Critic Ventures Alone in Pinter-Land', *Evening News*, 4 June 1965, p. 8.

Benedictus, David, 'Pinter's Errors', *The Spectator*, 11 June 1965, pp. 755, 758.

Brien, Alan, 'In London: *The Homecoming*. An Unnerving Horror-Comic Skill', *Vogue*, 15 September 1965, p. 75.

Browne, E. Martin, 'A First Look Round the English Theatre', *Drama Survey*, Summer 1965, p. 177.

Brustein, Robert, 'Thoughts From Home and Abroad', *New Republic*, 26 June 1965, pp. 29-30.

Bryden, Ronald, 'A Stink of Pinter', *New Statesman*, 11 June 1965, p. 928.

Bryden, Ronald, 'Fulfilments', *New Statesman*, 31 December 1965, pp. 1037-8.

Curtis, Anthony, 'Among Men', *The Sunday Telegraph*, 6 June 1965, pp. 10.

F.S., *'The Homecoming'*, Theatre World, LXI, 486 (July 1965), p. 19.

Gilliatt, Penelope, 'Achievement From a Tight Rope', *The Observer*, 6 June 1965, p. 25.

Hall, Stuart, 'Home Sweet Home', *Encore*, XII, 4 (July–August 1965), pp. 30-4.

Hobson, Harold, 'Pinter Minus the Moral', *The Sunday Times*, 6 June 1965, p. 39.

Holland, Mary, 'Home Lives', *Queen*, 16 June 1965, p. 15.

Hope-Wallace, Philip, 'Pinter's *The Homecoming* at the Aldwych' *The Manchester Guardian* 4 June 1965, p. 11.

'The Homecoming', The Listener, LXXIII, 1891 (24 June 1965), p. 936.

'The Homecoming ', Theatre World, LXI, 486 (July 1965), pp. 16-7.

Jones, D.A.N., 'Yorubaland', *New Statesman*, 16 December 1966, p. 916.

Kingston, Jeremy, 'Theatre', *Punch*, 16 June 1965, p. 901.

Kretzmer, Herbert, 'That Break Through Becomes a Cliche', *Daily Express*, 4 June 1965, p. 4.

Landstone, Charles, 'Revolts and Fascinates', *Jewish Chronicle*, 11 June 1965, p. 38.

Levin, Bernard, 'No Happy Homecoming for Mr. Pinter', *Daily Mail*, 4 June 1965, p. 16.

Lewis, Jack, 'Macabre', *Sunday Citizen*, 6 June 1965, p. 25.

Marriott, R.B., 'No Caretaker Needed in Harold Pinter's Sinister House', *The Stage*, 10 June 1965, p. 13.

Mortlock, C.B., *'The Homecoming'*, City Press, 25 June 1965, p. 11.

Nathan, David, 'Same Again from Puzzling Pinter', *The Sun*, 4 June 1965, p. 10.

'New Pinter Play for Aldwych', *The Times*, 27 January 1965, p. 14.

P.H.S., 'Pinter Axed', *The Times*, 9 October 1968, p. 10.

P.H.S., 'Thames Scrap Play on Legal Advice', *The Times*, 16 July 1971, p. 12.

P.H.S., 'The Making of a Book', *The Times*, 22 July 1968, p. 6.

Shorter, Eric, 'Outrageous and Gruesomely Funny Play', *Daily Telegraph*, 4 June 1965, p. 18.

Shulman, Milton, 'Drama — or Confidence Trick?' *Evening Standard*, 4 June 1965, p. 5.

Smith, Warren S., 'The New Plays in London, II', *Christian Century*, 8 September 1965, pp. 1096-7.

Spurling, Hilary, 'In His Own Write', *The Spectator*, 7 February 1969, p. 183.

Supple, Barry, 'Pinter's *The Homecoming*', *Jewish Chronicle*, 25 June 1965, pp. 7, 31.

Sutherland, Jack, 'Repellent Play from Pinter', *Daily Worker*, 5 June 1965, p. 2.

Taylor, J.R., '*The Homecoming:* a Pinter Power Struggle', *Plays and Players*, XII, 11 (August 1965), pp. 34-5.

Thirkell, Arthur, 'First Night', *Daily Mirror*, 4 June 1965, p. 18.

Trewin, J.C., 'Mr. Pinter Says That There's No Place Like Home', *Illustrated London News*, 19 June 1965, p. 30.

Trewin, J.C., 'Plays in Performance', *Drama*, 78 (Autumn 1965), pp. 16-23.

Trussler, Simon, 'Lots of Sound and Fury', *Tribune*, 16 December 1966, p. 15.

Young, B.A., 'Pinter's *The Homecoming* Is Staged in London', *New York Times*, 4 June 1965, p. 38.

Young, B.A., '*The Homecoming*', *The Financial Times*, 4 June 1965, p. 26.

'A World Out of Orbit', *The Times*, 4 June 1965, p. 15.

The Homecoming: Other References

Barthel, Joan, 'If You Didn't Know, It Was By Pinter', *New York Times*, 1 October 1967, sec. 2.

Brustein, Robert, 'Saturn Eats His Children', *New Republic*, 28 January 1967, pp. 34-6.

Esslin, Martin, 'Orgien und Exzesse', *Theater Heute*, (August 1965), pp. 40-2.

Gilman, Richard, '*The Homecoming*', *New York Times*, 22 January 1967.

Hewes, Henry, 'Pinter's Hilarious Depth Charge', *Saturday Review*, 21 January 1967, p. 51.

Kaiser, Joachim, 'Der Fall Pinter: die Heimkehr in den Munchner Kammerspielen', *Theater Heute*, VII, 4 (1966), pp. 37-8.

'New York Picks Pinter Play', *The Times*, 10 May 1967, p. 1.

The American Film Theatre/Cinebill, vol. 1. no. 2: Harold Pinter's *The Homecoming*, New York, 1350 Publishing, 1973, 20 pp.

Tea Party on Television

Allen, Bill, 'What *The Tea Party* Meant', *Daily Worker*, 9 April 1965.

Anderson, Kari, 'Another Fine Play By Harold Pinter', *The Stage*, 1 April 1965, p. 12.

Anderson, Patrick, 'Pinter's *Tea Party*', *The Spectator*, (April 1965), pp. 440, 442.

Barnes, Clive, 'Pinter Play Looks at Man Searching for Place in Life', *Daily Express*, 26 March 1965, p. 4.

Black, Peter, 'T.V.', *Daily Mail*, 26 March 1965, p. 3.

C.B., 'Unhappy With the World', *Jewish Chronicle*, 2 April 1965, p. 54.

Cooke, Fred, 'Pinter', *Sunday Citizen*, 28 March 1965, p. 23.

Davis, Clifford, 'Provocative Pinter', *Daily Mirror*, 26 March 1965, p. 18.

Day-Lewis, Sean, 'Pinter's TV Plays', *Drama*, 98 (Autumn 1970), p.76.

'Disturbing Television Play by Pinter', *The Times*, 26 March 1965, p. 15.

Holmstrom, John, 'Rambler', *New Statesman*, 2 April 1965, p. 547.

Lane, Stewart, 'Pinter's Hero Loses Control of His Destiny', *Daily Worker*, 27 March 1965, p. 2.

Laws, Frederick, 'Drama and Light Entertainment', *The Listener*, 15 April 1965, p. 575.

Mitchell, Adrian, 'Pinter's Quiet Scream', *The Sun*, 26 March 1965, p. 16.

Purser, Philip, 'Sense of Occasion', *The Sunday Telegraph*, 28 March 1965, p. 15.

Richardson, Maurice, 'Paranoid's Progress', *The Observer*, 28 March 1965, p. 25.

Shorter, Eric, 'Pinter Hero Who Loses Confidence', *Daily Telegraph*, 26 March 1965, p. 19.

Wiggin, Maurice, 'I'll Let Mine Cool', *The Sunday Times*, 28 March 1965, p. 26.

Tea Party and The Basement On Stage

Barber, John, 'Pinter Nightmares of Invaded Privacy', *Daily Telegaph* 18 September 1970, p. 14.

Barker, Felix, 'Mr. Pinter's Puzzles Leave Me Guessing', *Evening News* 18 September 1970, p. 3.

Dawson, Helen, 'Fledglings in a Limbo', *The Observer*, 20 September 1970, p. 25.

Fuller, Peter, 'Pinter's Enigma', *City Press*, 24 September 1970, p. 12.

Hope-Wallace, Philip, 'Harold Pinter Double-Bill at the Duchess Theatre', *The Guardian*, 18 September 1970, p. 8.

Hurren, Kenneth, 'Familiar Ground', *The Spectator*, 26 September 1970, p. 341.

Lambert, J.W., 'Dogs Beneath the Skin', *The Sunday Times*, 20 September 1970, p. 29.

Lambert, J.W., 'Plays in Performance', *Drama*, 99 (Winter 1970), pp. 14-30.

Marcus, Frank, 'End of the Beginning', *The Sunday Telegraph*, 20 September 1970, p. 14.

Nightingale, Benedict, 'Outboxed', *New Statesman*, 25 September 1970, pp. 394-5.

Philips, Pearson, 'Another Look at Classic Pinter', *Daily Mail*, 18 September 1970, p. 10.

Shulman, Milton, 'Now You See It, Now You Don't', *Evening Standard*, 18 September 1970, p. 25.

Sutherland, Jack, 'Familiar Themes in Pinter Double Bill', *Morning Star*, 19 September 1970, p. 2.

Taylor, J.R., *'Tea Party* and *The Basement'*, *Plays and Players*, XVIII, 2 (November 1970), pp. 36-9.

Thirkell, Arthur, 'Theatre', *Daily Mirror*, 18 September 1970, p. 16.

Trussler, Simon, 'Students v. the Rest', *Tribune*, 2 October 1970, p. 15.

Wardle, Irving, 'Pinter Propriety', *The Times*, 18 September, 1970, p. 6.

Wells, John, 'Theatre', *Punch*, 30 September 1970, p. 483.

Whitemore, Hugh, 'Plays', *Queen*, October 1970, p. 97.

Young, B.A., *'The Basement* and *The Tea Party'*, *The Financial Times*, 18 September 1970, p. 3.

Landscape on Radio

Bailey, Paul 'Pinter Play', *The Listener*, LXXIX, 2040 (2 May 1968) p. 583.

Ferris, Paul, 'Pop Press Imitations', *The Observer*, 28 April 1968, p. 32.

Lewis Peter, 'Turn On, Tune In to Pinter's Magic', *Daily Mail*, 26 April 1968, p. 16.

P.H.S., 'Pinter — a New Play', *The Times,* 10 January 1968, p. 8.

Rundall, Jeremy, 'On the Beach', *The Sunday Times,* 28 April 1968, p. 53.

Tynan, Kenneth, 'Shouts and Murmurs', *The Observer,* 21 January 1968, p. 27.

Wade, David, 'New Poetry in Pinter', *The Times,* 26 April 1968, p. 9.

Landscape and Silence on Stage

'Landscape and Silence', The Stage, 3 July 1969, p. 1.

'New Pinter Play', *The Times* 22 March 1969, p. 19.

'New Plays. The Latest Pinters: Less Is Less', *Time,* XCIV (18 July, 1969), p. 67.

Barber, John, 'Hushed Pinter Plays With Elusive Themes', *Daily Telegraph,* 3 July 1969, p. 19.

Barker, Felix, 'Pinter Comes Up With a Disaster', *Evening News,* 3 July 1969, p. 5.

Barnes, Clive, 'Harold Pinter's Debt to James Joyce', *New York Times,* 25 July 1969, p. 34.

Billington, Michael, 'Persecution on the Plane', *The Times,* 3 July 1969, p. 13.

Bryden, Ronald, 'Pared to Privacy, Melting into Silence', *The Observer,* 6 July 1969, p. 22.

Cushman, Robert, 'Evidence and Verdict', *Plays and Players,* XVI, 11 (August 1969), pp. 26-7.

Cushman, Robert, 'Pinter's Mixed Double', *The Observer,* 21 October 1973, p. 38.

Dukore, Bernard F., 'The Royal Shakespeare Company', *Educational Theatre Journal,* (December 1970), pp. 412-4.

Frye, Clarence, 'Guaranteed', *The Times,* 9 December 1970, p. 11.

Ghose, Zulfikar, 'Ghose's London: a Velediction', *Hudson Review,* (Autumn 1969), pp. 378, 380.

Hobson, Harold, 'Paradise Lost', *The Sunday Times,* 6 July 1969, p. 52.

Holland, Mary, *'Landscape* and *Silence',* Queen (23 July - 6 August, 1969), p. 62.

Hope-Wallace, Philip, 'Pinter Plays', *The Guardian,* 3 July 1969, p. 10.

Hughes, Catherine, 'Pinter Is As Pinter Does', *Catholic World,* (December 1969), pp. 124-6.

Jones, D.A.N., 'Corruption', *The Listener,* 10 July 1969, pp. 60-1.

Kingston, Jeremy, 'At the Theatre', *Punch,* 9 July 1969, p. 74.

Kretzmer, Herbert, 'Up to Pinter's Larks — But Arid . . .', *Daily*

Express, 3 July 1969, p. 8.

Lambert, J.W., 'Plays in Performance', *Drama*, 94 (Autumn 1969), p. 14.

Marcus, Frank, 'Pinter: the Pauses That Refresh', *New York Times*, 13 July 1969, p. 8.

Marowitz, Charles, *'Landscape* and *Silence'*, in *Confessions of a Counterfeit Critic* (London 1973), pp. 163-5.

Nathan, David, 'Pinter on the Road to Nowhere', *The Sun*, 3 July 1969, p. 7.

Nightingale, Benedict, 'To the Mouth of the Cave', *New Statesman*, 11 July 1969, p. 457.

Norman, Barry, 'How to Get Nowhere in Style', *Daily Mail*, 3 July 1969, p. 10.

P.H.S., 'Shorter Pinter', *The Times*, 11 April 1970, p. 69.

Pinter, Harold, 'Guaranteed', *The Times*, 12 December 1970, p. 11.

Porter, Peter, 'Foreplay', *New Statesman*, 7 August 1970, pp. 159-60.

P.W.B., 'Disappointing Pinter', *The Stage*, 10 July 1969, p. 13.

Shulman, Milton, 'Mini Pinter', *Evening Standard*, 3 July 1969, p. 17.

Spurling, Hilary, 'Lust and Forgetfulness', *The Spectator* 12 July 1969, pp. 49-50.

Sutherland, Jack, 'Two New Plays By Pinter', *Morning Star*, 4 July 1969, p. 2.

Thirkell, Arthur, 'Why Silence Was Best . . . ', *Daily Mail*, 3 July 1969, p. 14.

Trewin, J.C., 'Pinter Parodies', *Illustrated London News*, 12 July 1969, p. 29.

Trussler, Simon, 'Farcical Tragedy', *Tribune*, 18 July 1969, p. 11.

Wardle, Irving, 'Pinter Theatrical Twins in Pools of Solitude', *The Times*, 4 July 1969, p. 7.

Young, B.A., *'Landscape, Silence'*, *The Financial Times*, 4 July 1969, p. 3.

Old Times on Stage

Barber, John, 'Pinter's *Old Times* Static But Gripping', *Daily Telegraph*, 2 June 1971, p. 12.

C.H., 'Harold Pinter's *Old Times'*, *Sunday Express*, 6 June 1971, p. 23.

Frame, Colin, *'Old Times'*, *Evening News*, 2 June 1971, p. 3.

Hewes, Hugh, 'Odd Husband Out', *Saturday Review*, 4 December 1971, pp. 20, 22.

Hewes, Hugh, 'The British Bundle', *Saturday Review* 11 September 1971, pp. 20, 54.

Hobson, Harold, 'Remembrance of Things Past', *The Sunday Times,* 6 June 1971, p. 29.

Hope-Wallace, Philip, 'New Pinter Play at the Aldwych', *The Guardian,* 2 June 1971, p. 8.

Hurren, Kenneth, 'These Foolish Things', *The Spectator,* 12 June 1971, p. 821.

Kingston, Jeremy, 'Theatre', *Punch,* 16 June 1971, pp. 826-7.

Kretzmer, Herbert, 'Pinter Caught Fast in a Rut', *Daily Express,* 2 June 1971, p. 14.

Lambert, J.W. 'Plays in Performance', *Drama,* 102 (Autumn 1971), pp. 12-30.

Lewis, Peter, 'The Woman in the Shadow. . . .', *Daily Mail* 2 June 1971, p. 23.

Mahon, Derek, 'Derek Mahon Discusses Pinter's New Play', *The Listener* 10 June 1971, pp. 764-765.

Marowitz, Charles, *'Old Times',* in *Confessions of a Counterfeit Critic* (London, 1973), pp. 184-8.

Nightingale, Benedict, 'Three's a Crowd', *New Statesman,* 11 June 1971, p. 817.

Say, Rosemary, 'Pinter Looks Back', *The Sunday Telegraph,* 6 June 1971, p. 14.

Sutherland, Jack, 'Pinter and the Past', *Morning Star* 3 June 1971, p. 2.

Taylor, J.R., *'Old Times',* *Plays and Players* XVIII, 10 (July 1971), pp. 28-9.

Thirkell, Arthur, 'Theatre', *Daily Mirror,* 2 June 1971, p. 18.

Trussler, Simon, 'Shifting Alliances', *Tribune,* 18 June 1971, p. 11.

Wardle, Irving, *'Old Times',* *The Times,* 2 June 1971, p. 6.

Young, B.A., *'Old Times',* *The Financial Times,* 3 June 1971, p. 3.

Monologue on T.V.

Clayton, Sylvia, 'Monologue', *The Daily Telegraph,* 14 April 1973, p. 15.

Fiddick, Peter, 'Monologue', *The Guardian,* 14 April 1973, p. 10.

Night on Stage

Barber, John, 'Plays Show Wedlock At Its Worst', *Daily Telegraph,* 10 April 1969, p. 19.

Cushman, Robert, 'A Case of Mixed Feelings', *Plays and Players,* XVI, 9 (June 1969), pp. 22-5.

Hobson, Harold, 'Funeral for Farce', *The Sunday Times*, 13 April 1969, p. 55.

Hope-Wallace, Philip, 'Mixed Doubles', *The Guardian*, 10 April 1969, p. 9.

Kretzmer, Herbert, 'Where Marriage Is a Prison Sentence', *Daily Express*, 10 April 1969, p. 12.

Lewis, Peter, 'An Exciting Menu of Brevity', *Daily Mail*, 10 April, 1969, p. 12.

'Mixed Doubles', *Stage and Television Today*, 10 April 1969, p. 8.

'New Pinter Play', *The Times*, 15 March 1969, p. 21.

1969, p. 12.

Nightingale, Benedict, 'Love Plays', *New Statesman*, 18 April 1969, pp. 561-2.

Shulman, Milton, 'Eight Sharp, Cynical Looks at the Unholiness of Marriage', *Evening Standard*, 10 April 1969, p. 6.

Thirkell, Arthur, 'Find Focus on Marriage', *Daily Mirror*, 10 April, 1969, p. 18.

Trewin, J.C., 'Fantastic Exploit', *Illustrated London News*, 19 April 1969, p. 33.

Wade, David, 'Pinter Cutting It Short', *The Times*, 16 September 1970, p. 13.

Wardle, Irving, 'From Comedy to Sombre Realism', *The Times*, 10 April 1969, p. 7.

No Man's Land on Stage

Barber, John, 'Richardson and Gielgud in Fine Partnership', *The Daily Telegraph*, 24 April 1975, p. 15.

Barker, Felix. 'Pinter Rubbish so Masterly', *Evening News*, 24 April 1975, p. 8.

Billington, Michael. *'No Man's Land* at the Old Vic', *The Manchester Guardian*, 24 April 1975, p. 10.

Billington, Michael. 'Pinter's *No Man's Land'*, *The Guardian*, 9 January 1976.

Billington, Michael and Nicholas de Jongh, (Discuss *No Man's Land)*, *The Guardian*, 25 June 1975, p. 10.

'Batting for Pinter', *The Times*, 7 June 1975.

Brodie, Kelvin. 'Is it the A to Z, or sex, maybe', *The Sunday Times* 25 May 1975.

Coveney, Michael. *'No Man's Land'*, *Plays and Players*, XII, 10 (July, 1975), pp. 22-23.

Cushman, Robert. 'Mr. Pinter's Spoonerism', *The Observer*, 27 April 1975, p. 32.

Davis, Victor. 'Searching for His Golden Touch, Sir Ralph at 72', *Daily Express*, 23 April 1975, p. 13.

Edwards, Sydney. 'News of the Arts', *Evening Standard*, 15 August 1975.

Elsom, John. 'Harold Pinter's Mud-Patch', *The Listener*, 1 May 1975 pp. 585-586.

Hobson, Harold. 'Living Together', *The Sunday Times*, 27 April 1975.

Hobson, Harold. 'Unanswered Questions', *The Sunday Times*, 4 May 1975.

Hobson, Harold. 'Delicate Situations', *The Sunday Times*, 30 November 1975.

Holloway, Ronald. *'No Man's Land* at the Thalia Theater, Hamburg', *The Financial Times*, 9 December 1975.

Hurren, Kenneth. 'A Conversation with Peeves', *The Spectator*, May 1975, p. 549.

Itzin, Catherin. 'Pinter Abandoning the 'Pinteresque', *Tribune*, 2 May 1975, p. 9.

Jongh, Nicholas de. *'No Man's Land'*, *The Guardian*, 23 July 1975, p. 10.

Kretzmer, Herbert. 'Kretzmer's Verdict on the New Shows', *Daily Express*, 25 April 1975, p. 12.

Lambert, J.W., 'Plays in Performance', *Drama* (Summer 1975), pp. 37-39.

Marcus, Frank. 'Pinter in Limbo', *Sunday Telegraph*, 27 April, 1975.

Morley, Sheridan. 'Twice Knightly', *Punch*, 30 April 1975.

'No Man's Land for West End', *The Times*, 18 June 1975, p. 11.

'Harold Pinter's *No Man's Land*', *Vogue*, July 1975.

Nightingale, Benedict. 'Inaction Replay', *New Statesman*, 2 May, 1975, p. 601.

'Pinter's Taxi to *No Man's Land*', *Evening Standard*, 11 July 1975.

Shorter, Eric. 'Joy to Eye and Ear *No Man's Land*', *Daily Telegraph*, 25 July 1975, p. 9.

Shulman, Milton. 'Word Game For Two. . . .', *Evening Standard*, 24 April 1975, p. 19.

'Spooner Goes West', *The Observer* (13 July, 1975), p. 21.

Thirkell, Arthur. 'Funny, Peculiar. . . .', *Daily Mirror*, 24 April 1975, p. 16.

Tinker, Jack. 'Maybe not His Most Profound — But Riveting', *Daily Mail*, 24 April 1975, p. 24.

Trewin, J.C., 'New Plays', *Lady*, 8 May 1975, also 7 August 1975.

Trewin, J.C., 'Arranging the Features and Actuality', *The Times*, 24 April 1975, p. 10.

Young, B.A., *'No Man's Land'*, *The Financial Times*, 24 April 1975.

THE SCREENPLAYS

Pinter People:

P.H.S. 'Cartoons from Pinter', *The Times*, 14 January 1969, p. 6.

Sweeney, Louise. 'TV: 'Pinter People' with Menace and Moog', *Christian Science Monitor*, 4 April 1969, p. 6.

Wardle, Irving. 'Pinter and the Pilate Posture', *The Times*, 6 July 1968, p. 19.

The Servant:

Baker, Peter. *'The Servant'*, *Films and Filming*, X, 3 (December 1963), pp. 24-25.

Coleman, John. 'Malice Domestic', *New Statesman*, 15 November 1963), 1963), p. 718.

Gilliatt, Penelope. 'The Masterful Servant', *The Observer*, 17 November 1963, p. 27.

Losey, Joseph. 'The Monkey on My Back', *Films and Filming*, X, 1 (October 1963), pp. 11, 54.

Losey, Joseph. *'The Servant'*, *Sight and Sound*, XXXIII, 2 (Spring 1964), pp. 66-67.

Oakes, Philip. 'Masterly Who's Whose', *The Sunday Telegraph*, 17 November 1963.

Taylor, J.R., *'The Servant* and *The Caretaker'*, *Sight and Sound*, XXXIII, 1 (Winter 1963), pp. 38-39.

The Pumpkin Eater:

Butcher, Maryvonne, 'Modern Love', *Tablet*, 18 July 1964, pp. 809-810.

Coleman, John. 'Pumpkin Pie', *New Statesman*, 17 July 1964, p. 97.

Dent, Alan. 'The Case of Non-Involvement', *The Illustrated London News* (August 1964), p. 170.

Hibbin, Nina. 'Pulling in Different Directions', *Daily Worker*, 18 July 1964, p. 20.

Lewis, Jack. 'When Love's Labour's Lost', *The Sunday Citizen*, 19 July 1964, p. 20.

Mallet, Richard. 'Cinema', *Punch*, 29 July 1964, p. 169.

Oakes, Philip. 'Putting up with Love', *The Sunday Telegraph*, 19 July 1964, p. 10.

Pacey, Ann. 'Marriage — Stripped to Its Tortured Heart', *Daily Herald*, 15 July 1964, p. 5.

Price, James. 'Words and Pictures', *London Magazine* (October 1964), pp. 66-70.

'The Pumpkin Eater', *Films and Filming*, X, 8 (May 1964), pp. 16-17.

Quigly, Isabel. 'Home Fires', *The Spectator*, 17 July 1964, p. 84.

Richardson, Gina. 'Alarms and Diversion', *Time and Tide*, 23-29 July 1964, p. 32.

Robinson, David. 'The Improved Pumpkin Eater', *The Financial Times*, 17 July 1964, p. 24.

Sale, James. 'Savage Success', *Queen*, 15 July 1964, p. 14.

Samuel, F.H., 'Clayton's Masterpiece', *Jewish Chronicle*, 17 July 1964 p. 32.

Wright, Ian. 'New Films in London', *The Guardian*, 17 July 1964 p. 32.

Wright, Ian. 'New Films in London', *The Guardian*, 17 July 1964 p. 7.

The Quiller Memorandum:

'Film Script by Pinter', *The Times*, 2 December 1965, p. 15.

Gow, Gordon, *'The Quiller Memorandum'*, *Films and Filming*, XIII, 4 (January 1967), pp. 29-30.

'Guiness for *Quiller Memorandum*', *Time and Tide*, 7-13 April 1966, p. 16.

Mallett, Richard. 'Cinema', *Punch*, 16 November 1966, p. 748.

'The Quiller Memorandum', *Films and Filming*, XIII, 4 (January 1967), pp. 12-13.

Accident:

Alpert, Hollis. 'Where It's Happening', *Saturday Review*, 24 April 1967, repr. in J.G. Boyum and A. Scott (eds.), *Film as Film: Critical Responses to Film Art* (Boston, 1971), pp. 26-28.

Barker, Felix. 'He's a New Kind of Hero', *Evening News*, 9 February 1967, p. 8.

Butcher, Maryvonne. 'Outrageous Fortunes', *Tablet*, 11 February 1967, p. 159.

Coleman, John. 'No Accident', *New Statesman*, 10 February 1967, p. 198.

Dent, Alan. 'Love among the Dons', *The Illustrated London News*, 25 February 1967, p. 34.

Gibbs, Patrick. 'The Softer Side of Oxford', *Daily Telegraph*, 10 February 1967, p. 19.

Gill, Brendan. 'Inside the Redoubt', *New Yorker* (April 1967), repr. in: *Film as Film . . . .*,pp. 36-37.

Gilliatt, Penelope. 'Accumulating a Calamity', *The Observer*, 12 February 1967, p. 24.

Hibbin, Nina. 'A Man's Film — But It Got Me in the End', *Morning Star*, 11 February 1967, p. 3.

Hinxmann, Margret. 'Films', *Queen*, 15 February 1967, pp. 20-21.

Hirschhorn, Clive. 'Masterly, This Story of Three Men and a Girl', *The Sunday Express*, 12 February 1967, p 22.

Houston, Penelope. 'Losey's Hand in Pinter's Gloves', *The Spectator*, 17 February 1967, p. 195.

Kaufman, Gerald. 'No Message', *The Listener*, 9 March 1967, p. 330.

Lewis, Jack. *'Accident'*, *The Sunday Citizen*, 12 February 1967, p. 16.

Mallett, Richard. 'Cinema', *Punch*, 15 February 1967, p. 241.

Milne, Tom.*'Accident'*, *Sight and Sound*, XXXVI, 2 (Spring 1967), pp. 57-59.

Powell, Dilys. 'View from a Death', *The Sunday Times*, 12 February 1967, p. 49.

Robinson, David. 'Tensions Below', *The Financial Times*, 10 February 1967, p. 27.

Robinson, Robert. 'Meeting of the Twain', *The Sunday Telegraph*, 12 February 1967, p. 12.

Roud, Richard. *'Accident'*, *The Manchester Guardian*, 9 February 1967, p. 5.

Roud, Richard. 'All Done without Mirrors', *The Guardian*, 9 February 1967, p. 5.

Samuel, F.H. 'Student Affairs', *Jewish Chronicle*, 10 February 1967, p. 26.

Sarne, Mike. *'Accident'*, *Films and Filming*, XIII, 7 (April 1967), pp. 4-5.

Sarris, Andrew. *'Accident'*, in: *Film as Film. . . .*, pp. 31-34.

Sarris, Andrew. 'Second Thoughts about *Accident'*, in: *Film as Film. . .* pp. 34-35.

Taylor, J.R. *'Accident'*, *Sight and Sound* (August 1966), pp. 179-184.

Taylor, J.R. 'The Losey Film Everyone Has Been Waiting For', *The Times*, 9 February 1967, p. 4.

Walker, Alexander. 'Dons and Lovers — Vicious When the Jealousy Starts', *Evening Standard*, 9 February 1967, p. 5.

The Go-Between:

Billington, Michael. 'Losey's *Go-Between'*, *The Illustrated London N News* (July 1971), p. 63.

'Diary Note', *The Times,* 17 July 1970, p. 13.

P.H.S. 'Losey/Pinter's *The Go-Between'*, *The Times,* 2 December 1968, p. 10.

Taylor, J.R. *'The Go-Between',* *Sight and Sound* (Autumn 1970), pp. 202-3.

Addenda

Dempster, Nigel, 'The Romantic Life-Style of Lady Antonia', *Daily Mail,* 30 July 1975, p. 3.

'Divorce: Lady Antonia Named', *Daily Mail,* 29 July 1975, p. 1.

Edwards, Sydney 'Pinter's Taxi to No Man's Land', *Evening Standard,* 11 July 1975, pp. 20-21.

Eilenberg, Lawrence I., 'Rehearsal as Critical Method: Pinter's *Old Times',* *Modern Drama,* XVIII, 4 (December 1975), pp. 385-92.

'Fraser Drives Off to See Lady Antonia', *Evening News,* 29 July 1975, pp.1   pp. 1, 2.

'Fraser Goes to See Lady Antonia', *The Sun,* 30 July 1975, p. 5.

Hagberg, Per Olof, *The Dramatic Works of Samuel Beckett and Harold Pinter: a Comparative Analysis of Main Themes and Dramatic Technique* (Diss. Gothenburg, 1972).

Hayman, Ronald, 'Gray, Pinter and Bates: a Triangular Alliance', *The Times,* 26 July 1975, p. 9.

'Hickey, William,' 'Lady Antonia Is Accused by Harold Pinter's Wife'', *Daily Express   Daily Express,* 29 July 1975, p. 1.

'Hickey, William,' 'Pinter Drama, Act II: Playwright Says: Wife Told Me She Would Not Talk', *Daily Express,* 30 July 1975, p. 7.

Jackson, John; Jack Lewis, Margaret Hall, 'As Playwright Might Have Written Himself. Act One: The Lady Vanishes', *Daily Mirror,* 30 July 1975, p. 3.

Jenkins, Valerie, 'Women Like This Don't Have to Cast Spells', *Evening Standard,* 29 July 1975, pp. 1, 32.

'Lady Antonia Is Named in a Love Riddle', *Daily Mirror,* 29 July 1975, p. 1.

'Lady Antonia Named as "Other Woman"', *Daily Telegraph,* 30 July 1975, p. 13.

Owen, Michael, 'Pinter May Miss First Night', *Evening Standard,* 30 July 1975, p. 4.

Rook, Jean, 'So Full of Passion and Drama — Fiery Vivien's New Role', *Daily Express,* 30 July 1975, p. 3.